Introduction

to

Decumbiture

Wanda Sellar

The Wessex Astrologer

Published in 2014 by
The Wessex Astrologer Ltd,
4A Woodside Road
Bournemouth
BH5 2AZ
www.wessexastrologer.com

© Wanda Sellar 2014

Wanda Sellar asserts the moral right to be recognised as the author of this work.

Cover Design by Jonathan Taylor

A catalogue record for this book is available at The British Library

ISBN 9781910531006

Charts created using
Solar Fire © Esoteric Technologies Pty. Ltd and Astrolabe Inc.

Information contained in this book is for interest only and does not constitute medical advice.

No part of this book may be reproduced or used in any form or by any means without the written permission of the publisher.
A reviewer may quote brief passages.

To Ayako Berg, in Tokyo, whose encouragement and help was the inspiration to write this book

Other books by Wanda Sellar:

The Consultation Chart: A Guide to What it is and How to use it
An Introduction to Medical Astrology

Contents

1	An Introduction	1
2	The Houses	5
3	The Zodiac Signs	11
4	The Planets	18
5	Planetary Strength and Weakness	28
6	Fixed Stars and Azimene Degrees	35
7	Antiscia, Arabic Parts and Midpoints	40
8	Aspects	48
9	The Constitution	52
10	Illness	59
11	The Physician	63
12	The Terminal Triangle	66
13	Physic	71
14	The Humours	76
15	Timing and Length of Disease	83
16	Plants, Aromatics and Astrology	90
17	Material Medica	97
18	Steps to Judgement	127
19	Case Histories	135
20	Pet's Corner	150
21	Terminal Cases	159
22	Famous Decumbitures	167
	Conclusion	183

Abbreviations for books referenced in order of appearance:

CA   Lilly, Wm. *Christian Astrology*, Regulus, 1647.
AJD   Culpeper, N. *Astrological Judgement of Diseases from the Decumbiture of the Sick*, 1655, Astrology Classics.
CH   Culpeper, N. *The Complete Herbal and English Physician Enlarged*, Meyerbooks, 1997.
AG18   Morin Jean-Baptiste, *Astrological Gallica, Book Eighteen. The Strengths of the Planets*, translation from Spanish 2004, AFA.
BI   Al Biruni 1029 AD, *The Book of Instruction in the Elements of the Art of Astrology*.
EMA   Cornell, H.L. *Encyclopaedia of Medical Astrology*, Weiser, 1972.
TEMP Greenbaum, Dorian Giesler. *Temperament, Astrology's Forgotten Key*, The Wessex Astrologer, 2005.
AA   Bonatus, Guido. *The Astrologer's Guide or Anima Astrologiae*.
CM   Tobyn, G. *Culpeper's Medicine*, Element Books, 1997.
HAR   Barclay, O. *Horary Astrology Rediscovered*, Whitford Press, 1990.
CSI   Ebertin R. *Combination of Stellar Influences*, AFA, 1972.

1

An Introduction

The true crisis is best of all taken from that moment of time when first the sickness invaded the infirm.
'Christian Astrology', William. Lilly, p.291

Grounds for Decumbiture
That someone might remember to look at their timepiece at the onset of illness, more particularly at the time of taking to their bed, would show a remarkable presence of mind. But this is the foundation of the technique of decumbiture in astrology. Indeed, the expression 'decumbiture' derives from the Latin *decumbere*, meaning 'to lie down'. The process of lying down is more likely symbolic of the vital spirits or the life force no longer burning so brightly or flowing so freely, and that there was a need for recuperation, and almost inevitably the services of a physician.[1] If the physician was also an astrologer, he might set up a horoscope for the moment the patient took to his bed, and judge it accordingly.

It was also possible to apply decumbiture rules to a chart drawn up for the moment a patient took a vial of his urine to the physician/doctor.

Accept of that time when the sick parties Urine was first carried to somebody, to enquire of the disease, whether the party enquired of was physician or not.[2]

The inspection of urine (uroscopy) was a routine procedure amongst those who practised physic, and was thought to indicate the performance of body fluids, important in humoural medicine. Physicians who specialised in urine examination were colloquially referred to as 'pisse prophets'.[3]

The time of meeting between patient and physician could also constitute a valid decumbiture chart, which may have been a likely choice in most instances, since not everyone would have possessed a timepiece or have the presence of mind to run out into the garden and consult the sundial. Or indeed, thought of taking their urine to the physician.

Quite possibly, any breakdown in health or enquiry into a health matter does constitute credible grounds for the erection of a decumbiture chart, so it is quite likely that such a chart not only refers to the time a person takes to his or her bed, but also to any situation where there is a possible disruption of the life force. Culpeper mentions various occasions where decumbiture charts are drawn up for reasons other than succumbing to a supine position.

He examines a chart for the moment where a 60-year-old man has been run through with a sword causing injury to his arm.[4] Another chart describes a similar sword wound to a young man's knee. Not a likely occurrence these days, but injury with a knife could of course occur. Another chart describes someone falling sick whilst travelling. We may consider various possibilities upon which a decumbiture may be erected:

    a) Accidents
    b) A fall
    c) Sting by insect
    d) Heart attack
    e) IVF treatment
    f) Patient arriving for any kind of therapeutic treatment
    g) Waiting for results of a medical test
    h) Horary questions about one's own health, or that of another
    i) Entering a convalescent or nursing home
    j) An epidemic

Astrological Judgement

Astrologers William Lilly (1602-1681) and Nicholas Culpeper (1616-1654) recommend rules of delineation which may appear formulaic, but judgement rests with the astrologer, as always. Some of the aphorisms (truths or maxims) associated with this form of astrology may seem as if they are absolute pronouncements of certainty, but in fact they may only indicate possibilities rather than probabilities.

The decumbiture chart enables the astrologer/physician/therapist to help the client/patient deal with their condition, indicate a possible outcome, to monitor their feelings, make helpful suggestions and if the therapist is properly qualified, outline a course of treatment, orthodox or complementary.

The popularity of the decumbiture chart was at its height seemingly in the 17th century when herbs constituted the prescribed method of treatment, but it would appear that essential oils, as used in aromatherapy today, were also available, as well as minerals. Culpeper mentions the use of essential oils and minerals in his herbal.[5] Minerals or crystals were often used internally, *not* a method anyone would advocate in present times! (Like some plants, they can be toxic.)

The usual therapeutic use of minerals these days is through crystal healing, a therapy which purportedly has an effect on the subtle bodies and the meridians, which wasn't apparently taken into account in times gone by.

Naturally, to suggest medications, the astrologer should also be a qualified practitioner in a recognised therapy; nevertheless, the decumbiture chart can still be a useful aid in helping the astrologer to understand the genesis, and possibly predict the outcome of the condition.

In the past, with little regulation in medical matters, prescribing medicines in accordance with an astrological chart, and even diagnosing the disease, was not deemed unethical. Even predictions of death seemed to be a normal occurrence. Indeed there are many astrological aphorisms which warn of the impending presence of the grim reaper.

Where astrologers are not doctors, caution is necessarily exercised in making a definite diagnosis of illness and whether it is likely to be fatal or not. It would be more advisable for the astrologer to pinpoint areas of the body which may be subject to weakness, as well as inform on critical days, rather than be too definite about naming a particular disease.

The method of charting the progress of illness is one of the most useful aids in a decumbiture, if the client/patient attends regularly for treatment. If the condition is acute, minor, and brief (clears up after a month), it is judged by the transit of the Moon. For chronic conditions the Sun's movement is considered. Methodology is examined in the chapter on Timing and Length of Disease.

The decumbiture chart is basically an event chart, but since there is information sought, it links very well with horary astrology. The various strictures associated with horary are without doubt useful to contemplate in judgement, but should not obviate judgement as one might with a horary chart. For instance, an early or late degree rising does not deem that the chart is unfit to be judged, rather that the illness or condition is either at its inception or culmination, respectively. If the Moon is void of course (making no applying aspect to another traditional planet before leaving the sign), it does not mean that 'nothing will happen', rather that the condition will not change for better or for worse in the near future. It is a subtle difference, and even a helpful pronouncement, or indeed, the reverse!

Rules of delineation, strictures and aphorisms are given for guidance and as helpful aids for the astrologer's own judgement. Above all, it is imperative to keep the patient positive, as far as possible.

In the first instance the chart is judged by examining the seven traditional planets (Moon, Mercury, Venus, Sun, Mars, Jupiter, and Saturn) and the Ptolemaic aspects (conjunction sextile, trine, square and opposition), thereafter other aspects and outer planets might be considered.

A Question of Time

An occurrence such as a fall, an operation or an accident may have designated moments of time, so no question arises about validity. Some astrologers practising decumbiture prefer to set up a chart for the moment someone may telephone (or some other relevant means of communication) for an appointment. Other astrologers prefer to use the actual meeting in the consultation room. Which is right? There is no easy answer. Perhaps whatever works for the individual astrologer, or whatever seems apposite for the situation in question.

Revision
1. What does the Latin expression *decumbiture* mean?
2. What might the inspection of urine reveal?
3. Name three occasions where there might be a disruption of the life force.
4. Name three ways in which a decumbiture chart can enable the astrologer to help their client.
5. What originally constituted the main form of *Materia Medica* in regard to decumbiture charts?
6. Would it be advisable to recommend medications if not properly qualified?
7. Which planet governs the progress of acute conditions?
8. Which planet governs the progress of chronic conditions?
9. What might an early degree on the Ascendant suggest in a decumbiture chart?
10. What would a void of course Moon mean in a decumbiture chart?

References
1. CA, p.270.
2. CA, p.243.
3. Porter Roy. *Quacks*, Tempus, 2000, p.181.
4. AJD, p.112 onwards.
5. CHE, pp.205, 254, 353.

2

The Houses

O Heaven! Were man but constant, he were perfect.
'The Two Gentlemen of Verona', Act 5, Scene 4, William Shakespeare

Naturally all houses play their part in the delineation of a decumbiture chart, but certain houses are particularly significant.

The *1st house* is of prime importance simply because it relates to life, and describes the constitution. After the cosmic links to the 1st house have been judged, then attention should be given to the *6th house*. The houses may be examined in the following order, though this is not a strict rule, since other houses may be drawn into the process of delineation.

1st	The Constitution
6th	The Illness, or Condition
7th	The Physician
10th	The Medicine
4th	The End of the Matter
8th	Crisis, Death
12th	Hospitalisation

A Brief Description of the 12 Houses

First House: This house is first in importance since it represents the physical body, and life, and reveals the strength or weakness of the physical constitution at the time of illness. It may or may not reflect the strength or weakness of the physical constitution in the natal chart. If there is strong similarity, the current illness may be a genetic one, or a long standing one, though this is only conjecture.

The physical body in its entirety, the head and its structures (that is the brain) and important glands, belong to this house.

Mercury has joy in this house, and if dignified indicates resilience due to a strong flow of the life force. If debilitated, the patient's mental state may not be conducive to recovery and methods of support, psychological or medical, may need to be employed.

Second House: The neck, throat and all the internal structures in this area are governed by this house. It also describes the store of vitality, referred to as prana or life force or vital spirits. Its physiological counterpart is the thyroid, one of the endocrine glands, which regulates the body's energy levels. The thyroid gland regulates metabolism, the collective term for chemical processes in the body. It therefore governs the homeostatic balance of the body.

Third House: This is the house of duality, referring to the lower mind which is represented by the central nervous system (CNS) and peripheral nervous system (PNS). Each system has sensory and motor nerves but with different functions. The CNS involves the brain and spinal cord. The PNS connects the brain and spinal cord with the outlying regions of the body. This house also rules the arms, shoulders, hands and lungs.

The Moon has joy in this house, her fluctuating nature emphasising the inherent duality of the house and the dual nature of the nervous system.

Fourth House: Although family matters, genetic links and the home and environment may play a part in decumbiture, this house area tends to symbolise the end of the matter, or the grave in dire circumstances. It is therefore sometimes also symbolic of death as is the 8th house. Physical counterparts include stomach, armpits, and the lungs.

Fifth House: These days the fifth is seen as a house of creative expression that need not necessarily involve childbirth. The individual is conscious of his needs and his attitudes may involve self-centred interests that focus on pleasure. Pleasure linked to taverns and theatres, and other 'dens of iniquity', where disease of a venereal kind is likely to be contracted, apparently! Its physical counterpart involves the heart, back and liver.

We can see how Venus, the planet of love, has her joy in this house.

Sixth House: The current condition, sickness, and how strongly it may hurt the patient, is described by this house. The 6th is thought to rule the humoural perspective, in so much as whether there is a surfeit of any humour at the time of the decumbiture. Physical counterparts include intestines, kidneys, and physiological breakdown generally.

It is the joy of Mars, which threatens to disrupt the flow of the life force, and affect the health if badly placed.

Seventh House: The physician was represented by this house, and the efficacy of his or her diagnostic and treatment ability. Doctors are often taught that the most important 'medication' you can give to the patient is 'yourself', most likely in matters of understanding and compassion. Planets here oppose the Ascendant, which may create problems between patient and doctor.

If setting up a decumbiture chart for yourself, you should be beware of the Ascendant ruler's presence in the 7th house. This is a detrimental position since it opposes the Ascendant, and gives warning against being one's own physician. An alternative opinion would be advised. Physical counterparts include kidneys, navel and the womb.

Eighth House: This house describes the gravity of the situation and the breakdown of physiological processes. Not to mince matters, it rules death, and in past astrological practice there was no reticence, or so it appears, in pronouncing the imminent approach of the grim reaper. Times change and obviously such a pronouncement would not now be ethical.

Physical counterparts include genitals, urinary system and reproductive system. Otherwise, this house indicates crisis, peril, danger, surgery, cutting and toxicity as well as poisons.

Ninth House: The house of the higher mind, the link to God. It is interesting that mental aberration, or madness, was once thought to be linked to the divine. The higher mind illuminates and conveys information to the lower mind.[1] Sometimes the route is not a straightforward one, and delusions can result. Physiological counterparts are the thighs, hips, lower limbs and legs generally.

The Sun, which commands the life force, has joy in this house. A dignified Sun will aid the constitution and physiologically speaking this will indicate a strong heart.

Tenth House: Medication is shown by this house, which was often in the form of herbs, or 'chymical oils' (essential oils), even minerals. Culpeper does propose alternative methods by which medications might be chosen (see chapter on Physic). Physiological counterparts include the skeletal system and knees.

Eleventh House: The house which refers to friends and groups also has its counterpart in physiological 'groups' like blood cells and nerve cells. There may also be a link to the chemical/electrical transmitters linking the nerve cells across the synapses. Partner's children, or partner's fecundity, is also shown here. Physiological counterparts refer to calves and ankles.

Jupiter has joy in this house, which will aid recovery if dignified, since it has a reputation as a protective influence.

Twelfth House: The possibility of confinement and hospitalisation would be the main purpose of this house if emphasised in the decumbiture, as well as a chronic limitation on life, mental or physical. But it may also suggest epidemics, or one's destiny somehow linked to the masses, such as perishing in great disasters like earthquakes, plane crashes or mass drowning.[2] Emphasis on this house once suggested that a hex or spell had been put on the person to make them ill, which today might be seen as psychological illness, or psychosomatic illness. Physical counterparts include the feet and the immune system.

Saturn has joy in this house, and according to Lilly "*Saturn is author of mischiefe*", perhaps suggesting the planet's penchant for causing injury. [3]

Fortunate Houses
The 1st, 5th, 9th and 11th houses are deemed fortunate, or life-maintaining since they create fortunate aspects (trines and sextiles) to the Ascendant (life). Planetary significators placed here stand a better chance to rally the life force, but naturally everything depends upon the strength of the planet in terms of dignity or debility, as well as aspects.

Unfortunate Houses
The 6th, 8th and 12th weaken the health apparently, or at least the life force does not function at optimum strength. But this may be ameliorated by factors such as planetary strength for instance, or good aspects from the Fortunes (Jupiter and Venus).

Houses and Mode of Energy
Those houses termed angular, succedent and cadent describe a particular flow of the life force. Angular houses are said to be the strongest, followed by succedent houses and lastly cadent houses.[4]

Angular houses:	1/7, 4/10	– flowing, active energy
Succedent houses:	2/8, 5/11	– entrenched energy
Cadent houses:	3/9, 6/12	– vacillating energy

Naturally there are always modifications and permutations. For instance, whilst we deem the 7th an angular house, allowing an unimpeded flow of energy or the life force, it may not be conducive to a productive situation if malefic planets are situated there, particularly if they oppose the Ascending degree. In the same way, the 4th house, an angular house, refers to the grave.

The Sun and Moon in cadent houses are deemed to be weaker than other placements, yet the Sun has its joy in the 9th house and the Moon has its joy in the 3rd house. Contradictions abound but if planets are dignified by sign and aspect, it would probably ameliorate the supposed weakness of the cadent houses.

Important significators may be weakened if in weaker houses than the malefics, for instance the ruler of the Ascendant in a cadent house, and Saturn or Mars angular.

The Turned Decumbiture Chart
A chart may be 'turned' when the client is concerned about someone other than themself. This often takes the form of an horary question, though the rules of delineation are the same. The house relating to the person asked about becomes the 1st house. For instance, if it is the partner who is asked about, then the 7th house becomes this partner's 1st house, the 8th becomes this partner's 2nd house, and so on.

Or, should a question be asked about a parent, the mother for instance, then the 10th house becomes the mother's 1st house, and the 11th house becomes the 2nd house, and so on. The degrees on the cusp of the new Ascendant in a turned chart are now subject to aspects from planets.

The turned chart can be read from both the radix and turned point of view. Both interpretations may apply, though this process can be confusing! At first, at least.

Note: If a client presents a chart to an astrologer with the time taken from the moment the other party first took sick, or visited a physician, or any situation which involved a challenge to the life force, this would *not* constitute a turned chart, since the other party was directly involved in the event. A subtle difference.

> *If no urine or consent of the sick party come to the physician then the Ascendant presents the Querent (patient), but the person and the sickness must be required according to the relation the Querent hath to the sick party: a man for his Servant the sixth shall show his person, not his disease, that must be from the sixth to the sixth, which is the eleventh.* [5]

Revision
1. Which two houses are of prime importance in a decumbiture chart?
2. Which house might reveal the store of vitality or prana?
3. Which house rules the grave?
4. What does the Ascendant ruler placed in the 7th house, warn against?
5. Which house rules poisons?
6. Which house is the joy of Jupiter?
7. Which house might be linked to epidemics and disasters on a large scale?

8. Which houses are deemed unfortunate?
9. How does the life force flow in cadent houses?
10. Which house is the joy of Venus?

References
1. Bailey A. *The Soul, The Quality of Life*, Lucis Press, 1974.
2. Millard M. *Astrology and Medicine Newsletter*, No. 25, 1999.
3. CA, p.56.
4. AG18, p.91.
5. CA, p.283.

3

The Zodiac Signs

No patient can possibly be cured by the industry of his physician, be he never so learned, without the benevolent configuration of the stars.
'Christian Astrology', William Lilly, p.270

The Zodiac Signs and the Body

Aries – Head, Brain
Taurus – Neck, Throat
Gemini – Arms, Lungs
Cancer – Breasts, Stomach
Leo – Back, Heart
Virgo – Abdomen, Intestines
Libra – Lower back, Kidneys
Scorpio – Reproductive system
Sagittarius – Hips, Thighs
Capricorn – Knees, Skeleton
Aquarius – Ankles, Circulation
Pisces – Feet, Lymphatic System

ARIES
Element Fire
Gender Masculine
Quality Hot and Dry
Mode Cardinal
Timing Days

Aries rules the head and all the structures contained within it such as the brain and those linked to the nervous and endocrine systems. It also rules the face and all that it constitutes, such as the nose and mouth. However, each structure of the face and head does have specific planetary rulership, especially the eyes, which are ruled by the Lights (The Sun and Moon).

Conditions linked to Aries tend to be hot, acute and inflammatory, and include those diseases linked to the head as in brain disorders, mental disease, migraine, and skin disorders.

TAURUS
Element Earth
Gender Feminine
Quality Cold and Dry
Mode Fixed
Timing Years

Taurus rules the neck and all the structures contained within it such as the thyroid, one of the main endocrine glands which helps regulate the body's energy levels. This is the spiritual prana or vital force. It also rules the parathyroid, which helps to control the level of calcium in the blood, and affects function of nerves and muscles. Other structures include the trachea (windpipe), eustachian tube (connection between middle ear and nose) and the vocal chords.

Conditions linked to Taurus tend to be depression, diabetes, glandular swelling, goitre, gout, gum disease, laryngitis, mumps, palate disorders, swollen glands and constipation.

GEMINI
Element Air
Gender Masculine
Quality Hot and Moist
Mode Mutable
Timing Months

Gemini, a sign of duality, rules the two arms and hands, as well as ruling the lungs, the main organ of the respiratory system supplying the body with oxygen. It also rules the nervous system, which in two basic parts sets up a communication service between the organs of the body. It is divided into the central nervous system, and the peripheral nervous system.

Conditions linked to Gemini tend to be nervous conditions, memory loss, hearing, respiratory problems, blood diseases, anaemia, asthma, pleurisy, sinusitis, tuberculosis.

CANCER
Element Water
Gender Feminine
Quality Cold and Moist
Mode Cardinal
Timing Days

Cancer rules the softest parts of the body, the belly and the breasts. The digestive system comes under its rulership, particularly the stomach which lies on the left side of the abdomen under the diaphragm. The storage as well as the breakdown of food occurs here. Gastric juices in the stomach, such as the enzyme pepsin breaks down proteins, as well as hydrochloric acid which destroys the bacteria in food. There is also a link with the womb.

Conditions linked to Cancer include breast cancer, chest problems, flatulence, gastric problems, glandular disorder, oedema, phlegm, pigeon chest, shortness of breath, tuberculosis, ulcers.

LEO
Element Fire
Gender Masculine
Quality Hot and Dry
Mode Fixed
Timing Years

Leo has general rulership of the upper area of the body known as the thorax, which includes the heart, lungs and breastbone, though there is shared rulership with Gemini over the lungs, and Cancer over the breasts. Leo particularly rules the heart which pumps blood around the body, and the aorta, the large artery arising from the left ventricle of the heart and the *vena cavae*, the principle veins receiving deoxygenated blood. It rules the spine in general and the thoracic area (middle) of the back in particular.

Conditions linked to Leo include back problems, disorders of the heart, angina, hardening of the arteries, hypertension, pleurisy, spinal meningitis, tachycardia, sunstroke, vertigo.

VIRGO
Element Earth
Gender Feminine
Quality Cold and Dry
Mode Mutable
Timing Months

The digestive tract and the abdomen come under the general rulership of Virgo. This sign often gives a sensitive physique and allergies are common, especially those that are linked to food, since its main area of rulership covers the small and large intestines, referred to as the bowel. The intestines are linked to absorption of food and peristaltic action.

Conditions linked to Virgo include appendicitis, colic, Cholestasis, Crohn's disease, diarrhoea, dysentery, dyspepsia, flatulence, intestinal disorders, jaundice, malnutrition and worms.

LIBRA
Element Air
Gender Masculine
Quality Hot and Moist
Mode Cardinal
Timing Days

Libra rules the lumber region and the kidneys, which play a part in homeostasis, the maintenance of constant internal environment. The kidneys help to keep the body in balance by the process of secretion, excretion and elimination of toxins which are ultimately released in the urine. Further, Libra influences the balance between alkalinity, and regulation of temperature. There is a connection with the reproduction system and adrenals.

Conditions linked to Libra include adrenal problems, blood, Addison's disease, Bright's disease, corruption of blood, reproductive problems, skin diseases, syphilis, ulcers.

SCORPIO
Element Water
Gender Feminine
Quality Cold and Moist
Mode Fixed
Timing Years

Scorpio rules the reproductive system generally, including the womb, groin and prostate gland. It quite possibly rules the genetic code, the inherited instructions contained within the cells. This refers to chromosomes, the molecules containing deoxyribonucleic acid (DNA). Scorpio also rules the processes of elimination, the colon and anus as well as the genital-urinary system which includes the bladder and the urethra, as well as the nose, an organ of elimination.

Conditions linked to Scorpio are bladder infections, bow legs, constipation, cystitis, diverticulitis, enlarged prostate, gonorrhoea, gynaecological problems, impotence, irregular menstruation, prolapsed of womb, puerperal disorders and sterility.

SAGITTARIUS

Element	Fire
Gender	Masculine
Quality	Hot and Dry
Mode	Mutable
Timing	Months

Sagittarius rules the lower half of the body which includes the pelvis, the ring of bones enclosed by the coccyx and hip-bones. The pelvis protects the abdominal organs such as the bladder, rectum, and uterus. Sagittarius has overall rulership of the legs, but the thighs in particular. There is also an association with the liver, and the sciatic nerve.

Conditions include blood disorders, cramp, fistulas, itches, hip disorders, glycosuria (sugar in urine), lumbago, lung disease, mental illness, rheumatism and sciatica.

CAPRICORN

Element	Earth
Gender	Feminine
Quality	Cold and Dry
Mode	Cardinal
Timing	Days

Capricorn rules the skeletal system, the bones as living structures that constantly produce blood cells and interchange minerals with the blood. The knees are under its specific rulership. Apart from bones, Capricorn generally rules all hard substances like teeth, hair and nails. However, it also links into rulership of the skin, representing the body's boundary.

Conditions linked to Capricorn include rheumatism arthritis, disorders of bone growth, joint disease, stiff joints, bruises, calcification, cartilage trouble, chills, colds, congenital defects, constipation, depression, deafness and skin problems.

AQUARIUS
Element Air
Gender Masculine
Quality Hot and Moist
Mode Fixed
Timing Years

Aquarius rules the blood circulatory system, both the arterial and venous circulation, but in particular blood cells and ganglions, a group of nerves that have a common function. It rules the individual blood cells and cellular oxidation. Aquarius also rules individual nerve cells and possibly the electro-chemical transmission activating cells. The calves and ankles come under its rulership.

Conditions include anaemia, blood coagulation problems, breathing impairment, heart problems, lameness, nervous problems, restless legs syndrome, spastic conditions, toxaemia, and varicose veins.

PISCES
Element Water
Gender Feminine
Quality Cold and Moist
Mode Mutable
Timing Months

Pisces is linked to the immune system particularly the lymphatic system, which filters toxins from the body. This comprises the lymph nodes found in certain areas of the body, such as the chest, axillae and groin. The principal anatomic rulership is the feet, which according to the rules of reflexology reflect the whole body in miniature. Along with other water signs, Pisces rules the secretions and fluids of the body such as mucous and phlegm.

Conditions include addictions, allergies, catarrh, club foot, corns, deformities, dropsy, gout, feet and ankle swelling, forgetfulness, loss of muscular tone, oedema, and swollen glands and mental problems.

General indications
- Aries, Gemini, Leo, Libra, Sagittarius and Aquarius, the Fire and Air signs, are also known as masculine or diurnal signs, and generally speaking point to conditions that are easier to detect than the feminine or nocturnal signs, which include Taurus, Cancer, Virgo, Scorpio, Capricorn and Pisces, the Water and Earth signs. [1]

- Masculine signs relate to right side of the body, feminine to the left. [2]

Revision
1. Which sign rules the circulation in general?
2. Which sign contributes to the body's energy levels and which gland is responsible for it?
3. Name the three cold and moist signs.
4. With regard to timing, name the modes responsible for days, months and years.
5. Which two signs have rulership over the nose?
6. Which sign is linked to the lymphatic system?
7. Which side of the body do the masculine signs rule?
8. Which sign is linked to the liver?
9. Describe briefly the main function of the intestines, and name sign rulership.
10. Which sign is responsible for setting up a communication service between the organs of the body?

References
1. AJD, p.96.
2. ibid, p.96.

4

The Planets

Two stars keep not their motion in one sphere.
'King Henry IV', Part 1, Act 5, Scene 4, William Shakespeare

Planets and Physiology

Planets	Part of Body	Internal Organs	Blood
The Sun	Back	Heart	Heart
The Moon	Breasts	Stomach	Blood plasma
Mercury	Arms	Nervous system	Breath/oxygen
Venus	Lower back	Kidneys	Venous circulation
Mars	Muscles	Gall	Haemoglobin
Jupiter	Lower trunk	Liver	Arterial circulation
Saturn	Knees	Skeletal system	Platelets

The Senses [1]

Sight: the right eye to the Sun, the left to the Moon
(More specifically, the Moon rules the left eye of a man and the right eye of a woman, and the Sun rules the right eye of a man and left of a woman)
Hearing: Saturn
Taste: Jupiter
Smell: Mars
Touch and smell: Venus
The tongue and speech: Mercury

Vital Points

The most important planets always under consideration are those ruling the 1st and 6th houses, since they constitute the main significators. However, examination of the strength of the *Sun, Moon* and *Mercury* is important for the following reasons:

a) *The Sun* represents the heart and the source of the vital spirits. (It is interesting that the rotational axis of the Earth is tilted at 23½ degrees to the plane of its orbit around the Sun, and the heart is tilted 23½ degrees towards the centre of the body.)

b) *The Moon* also stands for the patient/client/querent. It rules the stomach, a vital organ, and monitors the progress of illness.

c) *Mercury* governs the *flow* of the vital spirits, as well as the mental state of the patient. A severely afflicted Mercury may indicate that the mind is disturbed, other factors considered.

In general where the Sun, Moon, Mercury and planetary ruler of the Ascendant are strong there is more hope of a cure, but if poorly dignified then the generation of the vital force is weakened. The Moon and Mercury are referred to as neutrals since they are fluctuating and adaptable, and take on the influence of sign position and close aspects.

The Sun

The Sun is the source of the vital spirits (life force, chi or prana) and signifies the body's vitality. Lilly states:

> *Have special consideration to the Luminary of the time (the Sun in day chart, the Moon in night chart) for according to the well or ill affection thereof you may improve your Judgement.* [2]

The hot and dry Sun warms the body and a strong Sun is indicative of a strong heart, or at least strong enough to withstand the disease. In general when the Sun, Moon and ruler of the Ascendant are free from the affliction of Saturn and Mars or the ruler of the 8th house, there is more cause for optimism.

An afflicted Sun prolongs disease. If the Sun, as well as the Moon, are positioned under the Earth, a difficult situation ensues since *"there is no light in this world without the Sun or the Moon."* [3]

In its pathological action the Sun causes inflammation. The Sun, as well as Mars, overheats the body. The Sun is both beneficent when in aspect and distant, and maleficent when in conjunction and near.[4] Planets in combustion (within eight degrees of the Sun) are weakened. It appears that if the Moon separates from combustion, the sickness increases until the Moon comes to the opposition of the Sun. This could indicate a crisis situation for good or ill. It may worsen if the Moon next aspects the ruler of the 8th house.[5]

If the Sun, as well as the Moon, are in cadent houses, and their dispositors are afflicted, this indicates a difficult illness unless the Fortunes intervene with beneficial aspects, especially if the Fortunes are stronger than the Infortunes.[6] A long illness ensues if both the Sun and the Moon are afflicted by Saturn, especially if the angles are involved.

If the Sun is author of the disease, in so much as it rules the Ascendant or 6th house, and is afflicted, diseases are likely to involve the heart and blood, or the brain and possibly the back. Chronic diseases are judged by the Sun.

The Moon
The Moon's importance in decumbiture rests mainly on two points:

1.   It is co-significator of the patient, and therefore its strength or weakness must be considered. The stronger the Moon at time of decumbiture, the more likelihood of speedy recovery. The Moon's strength should be judged along with that of the ruler of the Ascendant and the Sun.[7]

2.   The Moon monitors the progress of the disease, especially in acute conditions.[8]

The Moon's Strength

- Consider the zodiac sign in which the Moon is placed at decumbiture. Note the house, whether Moon is dignified, debilitated or peregrine, in a masculine, feminine, diurnal or nocturnal sign. Consider whether it is hot, dry, cold or moist and what part of the body it governs by sign.

- The Moon, being cold and moist, is comfortable in the Water signs (less so in Scorpio where it is in its fall), as well as Earth signs (less so in Capricorn where it is in its detriment). It is not very comfortable in Air, but its most difficult position is the hot and dry Fire signs,[9] the antithesis of its cold and moist nature.

- The Moon in Fire signs tends towards inflammation; in Watery signs, phlegm, in earth signs depression, in Air signs it affects the breath and blood.[10] If the Moon is in a fixed sign it indicates a long sickness; a cardinal sign quick resolution for good or ill, and in a mutable or double bodied sign, the disease will be very difficult to cure since the illness tends to waver.

- The most important consideration is the Moon's separating and applying aspects (translation of light), since this may indicate the part of the body under affliction, and the predominant humour. The basic premise is that if the Moon separates from a bad aspect to a weak, malevolent planet and applies to a strong fortunate planet, recovery is more likely.[11]

- Promise of good health occurs when a strong Moon applies to the Ascendant ruler with a trine or sextile, and is not afflicted by the ruler of the 6th or 8th houses.[12]

- If the Moon is square or in opposition to an Infortune, such as Mars, the disease is serious, but good aspects to Venus or Jupiter suggest the sick will recover.[13]

- Generally speaking, when the Moon is strong, fast in motion[14] and unafflicted, and in no aspect to the ruler of the 6th house, the patient has strength to fight the illness, other indications in the chart permitting.

- If the Moon aspects Venus and Jupiter, and neither rule the 8th house of death, the most grievous of maladies is remitted.[15]

Moon's Weakness

- If the Moon is author of the disease, in so much as it rules the Ascendant or the 6th house and is afflicted, diseases may involve the breasts, stomach and the fluids of the body including the blood plasma.

- The greatest difficulties involve a square or opposition to the Infortunes, particularly if the Moon is also in square or opposition to the Ascendant, or in difficult aspect to the rulers of the 6th, 8th or 12th house, as well as decreasing in light and being slow in motion.[16]

- It is also threatening to health if the Moon and the ruler of the Ascendant are in square, opposition, conjunct a retrograde Saturn or Mars, combust, slow in motion, peregrine, fall or detriment, or in the 6th or 8th or in any aspect with the lord of the 6th, 8th or 12th house.[17]

- If there is translation of light (separating from one planet and applying to another) from an afflicted dispositor of the Moon to the Lord of the Ascendant or the sign Ascending, the patient suffers according to the nature of the signs and planets signifying the illness.[18]

- The Moon besieged by the Infortunes (placed between Mars and Saturn, or the Sun with one of the malefics) indicates a very difficult situation.[19]

Lunations
Check the degree of the preceding eclipse and lunation.[20] If the Moon or ruler of the Ascendant is in conjunction, this is not favourable for health since they both represent the body.

The Moon loses power when waning and increases its power when waxing, either may help or hinder depending upon the situation. The Moon is cold and moist, and is said to increase in warmth as it waxes, and decreases in warmth as it wanes.

The New Moon at decumbiture may be critical as it could weaken the constitution; the Full Moon could bring a condition to fruition, for good or ill. At the Full Moon, there is a high tide of fluids and the New Moon brings low tide of fluids,[21] hence the rise and fall of fluids in the body. There is likely to be a plethora of fluids at the Full Moon, and less so at the New Moon, suggesting oedema or haemorrhage.

Void of Course Moon
Observe if the Moon is void of course (VOC): making no applying aspect to another planet before leaving the sign at the time of the decumbiture.

> *A planet is Void of Course when he is separated from a planet, nor doth forthwith, during his being in that signe, apply to any other.* [22]

If the Moon is definitely VOC, that is beyond the moiety of orbs to other planets, there is likely to be little change in the condition in the near future. As soon as the Moon begins to apply to a planet in the course of the illness, something changes for better or for worse in the condition of the patient.

> *When the Moon is Void of Course at Decumbiture but at the next crisis (when the Moon is square, opposition or conjunct Decumbiture Moon) it is sextile or trine Jupiter and/or Venus, there is greater hope of recovery.*[23]

If the transiting Moon crosses a sign barrier and is still VOC, then clearly something will change in the condition of the patient. It will depend how the Moon fares in the new sign. If it is in a sign where it can act unimpeded such as Cancer, its domicile, or in Taurus, its exaltation, the patient is more likely to improve. The Moon will feel less comfortable in Capricorn, its detriment, and in Scorpio, its fall. Though the Moon tends to feel comfortable in cold and moist signs, this may also increase the moisture in the body, depending upon the aspects the Moon makes.

Mercury

Mercury governs the flow of the vital spirits, as well as the breath and voice, which tend to be shallow and weak when the life force is deficient. The strength of Mercury in the decumbiture aids other signatures of recovery, but if afflicted recovery may be prolonged. In general where the Sun, Moon, Mercury and the planetary ruler of the Ascendant are poorly dignified, then the generation of the vital force is weakened.

Mercury and the Moon govern the two hemispheres of the brain, the left practical side and the right imaginative side respectively. If the Moon and Mercury are in difficult aspect to each other, the mind may be disturbed, particularly if the 3rd, 9th, 6th or 9th houses are involved. Lilly states:

Mercury unfortunate the sick party hath his brain disaffected, is disturbed with an unquiet fancy or minde with a frenzie, falling sickness, cough.[24]

Both Mercury and the Moon, often referred to as the neutrals, are fluctuating as well as adapting, and tend to reflect the activity/energy of the planet closest in aspect. Therefore, either planet can work for good or ill. In its natural state Mercury is said to be cold and dry, though this can change according to its position and aspects. For instance, if Mercury is in difficult aspect to Mars, the disease may come from anger,[25] and Mercury becomes hot.

If Mercury is the author of the disease, in so much as it rules the Ascendant or 6th house, and is afflicted, diseases are likely to involve the nervous system, the brain and the breath. It is possible that medications, perhaps in terms of herbs or essential oils, should be used to strengthen the planet and the areas of the body it represents.

The Two Fortunes: Venus and Jupiter
Venus like Jupiter governs moisture, but where Venus is cold, Jupiter is hot. If Venus is author of the disease, in so much as ruling the Ascendant or 6th house, and is afflicted, diseases are likely to involve the breasts, the genitals, venous blood circulation and the kidneys. If Jupiter is such author, diseases are likely to involve the liver and arterial circulation.

Nevertheless the two Fortunes have a beneficial effect upon the health. *"The Fortunes strive to maintain nature, the Infortunes to destroy. Judge which is the strongest when passing on the Decumbiture."* [26] Usually it is the stronger planet that overcomes the weaker, resulting in quick or slow recovery. *"The malevolents may threaten hard but the benevolents will stay the deadly blow."* [27]

Indeed if the Fortunes are stronger than the Infortunes in the Decumbiture chart, there is greater promise of recovery especially if they are in benevolent aspect to the Moon or Ascendant ruler. Jupiter for instance, strives to maintain health, whilst Saturn endeavours to destroy it.[28]

It appears that a trine from Jupiter to the Sun will ameliorate a situation as difficult as the ruler of the Ascendant applying to the ruler of the 8th house.[29] In the same way, a trine from Venus to the Moon will ameliorate the same situation,[30] as long as the Moon does not rule the 8th house. This situation has to be compared with the condition of the planetary ruler of the Ascendant, the stronger it is the better for the patient.

It seems that no matter how dire a situation appears, a benevolent aspect to an important significator from one of the Fortunes, such as the Ascendant or 6th house ruler, seems to ameliorate the severity of the condition:

When you find the Moon receded from opposition of the Sun, to be swift in motion and hastens to the square or opposition of Mars it will come to pass, that the disease which the Querent now undergoes will be grievous and mortal, but if he salute at the same time the sextile or trine of Jupiter or Venus, sick shall recover. [31]

It appears therefore, that if either of the Fortunes cast their beneficent rays in the direction of a difficult cosmic configuration, there is hope of speedy recovery, but perhaps less so if either Fortune rules the 8th house. In the same way, the strength of the Fortune should be noted. Culpeper suggests that squares and oppositions from the Fortunes are better than the sextiles and trines of the Infortunes. [32]

The Two Infortunes: Mars and Saturn

Mars and Saturn, traditionally referred to as the lesser and greater Infortunes respectively, tend to worsen the health, especially if they have more dignity in the chart than the Fortunes. In general both planets afflicting important significators, especially the rulers of the 1st and 6th houses, threaten severe illness. What makes the malefics malefic is that they possess excessive amounts of a quality.[33]

However, Mars or Saturn in benevolent aspect to Significators are not likely to be harmful unless the aspect is with reception.[34] Dignified Infortunes may on occasion actually be helpful![35] Discernment is needed here.

If either of the malefics are positioned in the 1st house, something may alter in the constitution.[36] This is particularly so if at the same time the Moon is in square or opposition to the Ascendant, or in difficult aspect to the rulers of the 8th, 6th or 12 houses, or decreasing in light and slow in motion.[37]

A difficult situation may be mitigated if either of the Infortunes exchange dignity with a Fortune (by sign and exaltation strongest, followed by trip, term and face). Significators appearing to be in good position but exchange dignity with an Infortune, weaken the situation. The Infortunes can spoil a hopeful situation.

Besiegement by the Infortunes indicates a difficult situation, especially if it's the Moon.[38]

The Infortunes tend towards dryness, and the Fortunes tend towards moisture. When Saturn afflicts the luminaries, the body loses heat, but when Mars afflicts the luminaries, the body may become feverish. Saturn is an enemy to both luminaries.[39]

If Mars is author of the disease, in so much as it rules the Ascendant or 6th house, and is afflicted, there may be problems with inflammation, fevers, burns, muscles, gall bladder and blood.

Saturn gives a tendency towards depression, and there may be problems with coughs, consumption (tuberculosis), problems with ears, teeth, bladder, gout and rheumatism. Saturn diseases are likely to be chronic, made worse by being in a fixed sign, as well as retrograde or slow in motion. Mitigation occurs if Saturn is in a cardinal sign and in any of his terms or swift in motion.

THE OUTER PLANETS

Uranus, Neptune, Pluto
In traditional astrology, the outer planets are not considered in judgement. The seven planets as well as the Ptolemaic aspects, take pride of place. Nevertheless, it may not always be wise to dismiss the outer planets or the modern aspects if they seem pertinent to judgement. Additional information may be gained if an outer planet is placed in a prominent position in the chart.

Outer planets that are in hard aspect to important significators, such as the Ascendant or 6th house ruler, and perhaps also to the Moon, the Sun and Mercury, may be significant.

Uranus is associated with synaptic transmission in the nervous system, and in pathological action may cause spasm and distort the flow of energy and blood, perhaps causing allergy. Disease may include those of the nervous system.
Neptune is associated with the water distribution in the body, and in pathological action will slacken tissues and make the blood sluggish with tendency to organ atrophy. Neptune symbolizes generalised weakness, and diseases could include those relating to the fluids of the body.
Pluto rules the organs of generation and in pathological action could change things at a cellular level. Pluto could well represent heart pacemakers and the effects of antibiotics.[40] The disease could include cellular problems.

Dragon's Head and Dragon's Tail (The Nodes)
Planets in the same degree as the Nodes are believed to show a fateful illness, however, it is possible that this may only compound an already difficult situation. Significators with South Node tend not to be beneficial to health, particularly if in the 6th house.[41] Conversely, the North Node in the 1st house augers well for health.

The Moon applying to the Nodes, presumably by difficult aspect, is not a good sign for health, but this does not seem to create similar problems if the Moon is separating from them.[42] Apparently the North Node brings warmth and the South Node creates a cold situation. Possibly the North Node increases the effects of both beneficent and maleficent planets.[43]

Revision
1. Which planet is said to be the source of the vital spirits?
2. Which planet is said to be the conveyor of the vital spirits?
3. If the transit Moon crosses a sign barrier and finds itself in exaltation, how might this affect the health?
4. Suggest two conditions that may occur at the Full Moon.
5. Which two planets are said to have a beneficial effect upon the health?
6. A Fortune brings beneficence, though lessened when it rules which house?
7. Describe what might be the reaction in the body if Mars is the author of the illness?
8. What happens to a planet besieged by Mars and Saturn?
9. Which planet is associated with synaptic transmission in the nervous system?
10. In which house does the North Node apparently contribute to good health?

References
1. CA, p.269.
2. ibid p.256.
3. ibid p.283.
4. *BI*, p.232.
5. CA, p.258.
6. ibid p.252.
7. ibid p.285.
8. AJD, p.68.
9. *EMA*, p.549.
10. AJD, p.37.
11. CA, p.270.
12. ibid p.255.
13. ibid p.252.
14. ibid p.252.
15. AJD, p.68.
16. CA, p.52.
17. ibid p.250-1.
18. ibid p.253.
19. AJD, p.109.
20. CA, p.266.
21. EMA, p.549.

22. CA, p.112.
23. ibid p.255.
24. ibid p.263.
25. AJD, p.91.
26. ibid p.106.
27. ibid p.104.
28. ibid p.106.
29. CA, p.285.
30. AJD, p.68.
31. CA, pp.252-3.
32. AJD, p.72.
33. TEMP, p.25.
34. CA, p.283.
35. AG, p.22.
36. AJD, p.107.
37. CA, p.252.
38. AJD, p.109.
39. ibid p.36
40. CM, p.153.
41. CA, p. 289.
42. AJD, p.110.
43. BI, pp.233-4.

5

Planetary Strength and Weakness

Examine the condition of the planets, whether in benevolent or malevolent signs; masculine or feminine, diurnal or nocturnal, hot, dry, cold or moist and part body they govern.

'Astrological Judgement of Diseases from the
Decumbiture of the Sick', Nicholas Culpeper, p.70

The strength or weakness of a planet is determined by its celestial state and its position in respect to the horizon. Assessing planets' strength or weakness is primarily determined by their essential dignities and debilities, as in the following table. Accidental dignities are judged by the strength gained by the planet other than its zodiacal position such as planetary joy and the speed of its motion.

Key to The Table of Essential Dignities (opposite)
Columns
1. Zodiac signs.
2. Day and Night domicile. When a planet is in exaltation it is strong and points to the resilience of the constitution and relevant physiological processes. In medical astrology, Day and Night (D/N) rulership respectively, indicates whether the condition is clear to see (day rulership) or obscure (night rulership). For instance Venus in Libra indicates a condition that is more apparent than that of Venus in Taurus, at least initially.
3. Exaltation. When a planet is in exaltation, it is likewise strong.
4. Triplicity of planets, day and night. A planet in triplicity, term or face, is also strong but less so than exaltation.
5. Terms of the planets. A planet in its own term adds some strength.
6. Faces of the planets. A planet in its own face adds a little less strength than terms.
7. Detriment A planet in its detriment and fall is weak, and as a prime significator, indicates the patient is vulnerable and does not have a great deal of strength to fight disease. Planets, and therefore the patient, may suffer if in terms of malevolent planets (Mars and Saturn).
8. Peregrine. The planet has no natural affinity in the sign, that is it is not in domicile, exaltation, triplicity, term or face, and its effect is weakened.

PTOLEMY'S TABLE OF ESSENTIAL DIGNITIES & DEBILITIES [1]

Sign	Dom	Ex	Tri	Terms					Faces			Det	Per
♈	♂ D	☉ 19	☉ ♃	♃ 6	♀ 14	☿ 21	♂ 26	♄ 30	♂ 10	☉ 20	♀ 30	♀	♄
♉	♀ N	☽ 3	♀ ☽	♀ 8	☿ 15	♃ 22	♄ 26	♂ 30	☿ 10	☽ 20	♄ 30	♂	
♊	☿ D	NN 3	♄ ☿	☿ 7	♃ 14	♀ 21	♄ 25	♂ 30	♂ 10	♃ 20	☉ 30	♃	
♋	☽ N/D	♃ 15	♂ ♂	♂ 6	♃ 13	☿ 20	♀ 27	♄ 30	♀ 10	☿ 20	☽ 30	♄	♂
♌	☉ D/N		☉ ♃	♄ 6	☿ 13	♀ 19	♃ 25	♂ 30	♄ 10	♃ 20	♂ 30	♄	
♍	☿ N	☿ 15	♀ ☽	☿ 7	♀ 13	♃ 18	♄ 24	♂ 30	☉ 10	♀ 20	☿ 30	♃	♀
♎	♀ D	♄ 21	♄ ☿	♄ 6	♀ 11	♃ 19	☿ 24	♂ 30	☽ 10	♄ 20	♃ 30	♂	☉
♏	♂ N		♂ ♂	♂ 6	♃ 14	♀ 21	☿ 27	♄ 30	♂ 10	☿ 20	♀ 30	♀	☽
♐	♃ D		☉ ♃	♃ 8	♀ 14	☿ 19	♄ 25	♂ 30	☿ 10	☽ 20	♄ 30	☿	
♑	♄ N	♂ 28	♀ ☽	♀ 6	☿ 12	♃ 19	♂ 25	♄ 30	♃ 10	♂ 20	☉ 30	☽	♃
♒	♄ D		♄ ☿	♄ 6	☿ 12	♀ 20	♃ 25	♂ 30	♀ 10	☿ 20	☽ 30	☉	
♓	♃ N	♀ 27	♂ ♂	♀ 8	♃ 14	☿ 20	♂ 26	♄ 30	♄ 10	♃ 20	♂ 30	☿	☿

Note that a planet in detriment or fall recovers some strength if it is of the same gender.[2] For instance if Saturn is in Aries, where it has its fall, or Saturn is in Leo, where it is in detriment; both the planet and the signs are masculine. If Venus is in Scorpio, both planet and sign are feminine.

Planets may gain strength through their house position and/or aspects. The situation is never so dire if the planet and the ruler of the sign are friends rather than enemies.[3] Given below is the state of friendship between the planets.[4] The importance of this in the overall judgement of the chart may be minimal, but it may be worth keeping in mind.

Friends and Enemies

Planets	Mutually hurtful with	Injurious to	Offering friendship to	Asking friendship from
Saturn	Sun & Moon	Jupiter	Mars	Venus
Jupiter	Mars & Mercury	Mercury	Venus	Moon
Mars	Jupiter & Venus	Moon	Sun	Saturn
Sun	Saturn	Venus	–	Mars
Venus	Mars & Mercury	–	Saturn	Jupiter
Mercury	Jupiter & Venus	Venus	–	–
Moon	Saturn	Mars	Jupiter	Venus

Planetary Joys

Strength is attributed to planets when placed in the following houses:

The Moon rejoices in the 3rd house
Mercury rejoices in the 1st house
Venus rejoices in the 5th house
The Sun rejoices in the 9th house
Mars rejoices in the 6th house
Jupiter rejoices in the 11th house
Saturn rejoices in the 12th house

Quite often there is a mixture of designated strengths, for instance a planet may be dignified by sign but weak by house, or vice versa. Judgement may in such a case show the body rallying by intermittent measures.

A planet within five degrees of a house cusp is already deemed to be in the next house, or at least of important influence. A planet closest to the house cusp will act more effectively in the essential matters of that house, than one placed in the middle.[5] Though not all influence is lost from the house it still physically occupies, as is often thought.[6]

Planetary Motion

More information on the state and course of the disease or condition can be gained by noting the mean or average motion of a planet through 24 hours. Subtract the longitudinal positions of the planets at noon from those of the following day at noon. Below is a table giving the mean motion of the seven traditional planets.

Mean Motion of Planets

PLANET	DEGREES	MINUTES	SECONDS
☽	13 degrees	10 minutes	35 seconds
☉	0 degrees	59 minutes	08 seconds
☿	1 degrees	23 minutes	8 seconds
♀	1 degrees	12 minutes	0 seconds
♂	0 degrees	31 minutes	27 seconds
♃	0 degrees	4 minutes	59 seconds
♄	0 degrees	2 minutes	01 seconds

Planets in order of speed:
Moon, Mercury, Venus, Mars, Jupiter, Saturn, Uranus, Neptune, Pluto

Since the planets move in an elliptical orbit around the Sun, motion is at some times accelerated and at other times slowed down in ratio to their distance from the gravitational centre. A planet travels faster than its mean motion when it passes through fewer degrees in transit through 24 hours. For instance, the Sun's daily mean motion is 0 degrees and 59 minutes. If it were to travel 58 minutes through 24 hours, then it would be said to be travelling faster than its mean motion, which is generally more favourable to health. A slow-moving planet will suggest a sluggish flow of the vital spirits.

However, if the overall tone of the chart suggests a weakened constitution and little hope of recovery, then a fast travelling planet may hasten the demise of the patient.

Slow in Motion A planet travelling slower than its mean motion in 24 hours tends to prolong sickness, often due to a sluggish metabolism.[7]

Fast in Motion A planet travelling faster than its mean mtion in 24 hours tends to speed up illness to its conclusion.

A *Stationary* planet hinders improvement, and has "time to make mischief".[8] It may also suggest sluggish life force, or congestion.

A *Retrograde* planet, which appears to be going backward in motion when decreasing in longitude as viewed from the Earth, can create difficulties. Or interruption in health or treatment, or lack of completion.[9] It may describe a lingering illness, or threaten relapses[10] or change of temperature.[11]

Nevertheless retrograde motion is not always negative. If a planet turns retrograde when applying to a threatening significator (ruling the 8th house for instance), this may prevent the perfection of a testing situation.

It is worth observing the movements of the planets in the ensuing days of the illness or condition, to see whether the planets are about to retrograde or become stationary. Stationary planets might be about to become retrograde after the first station, or about to become direct in motion after the second station.[12] Naturally, planets about to become retrograde will slow down the illness, condition or situation; becoming direct will speed up illness towards conclusion.

It is also important to monitor the movement of the planets under consideration in respect of sign change and their welfare in a particular sign as this could affect the patient in terms of strength or weakness.

Besiegement

A planet gains strength if placed bodily between Venus and Jupiter and decreases in strength if placed bodily between Mars and Saturn. It may be worth making a note of other types of besiegement, such as between a malefic and the Sun, or if placed between outer planets. "*The Moon besieged by the Infortunes or between Sun and Mars, or between Sun and Saturn, are ill omens of health.*"[13]

Cazimi

A planet within 17 minutes of conjunction to the Sun is in 'the heart of the Sun' and supposedly gains strength, though not everyone thinks so!

Combustion/Sunbeams

A planet within 8 degrees 30 minutes of the Sun, whether applying or separating, is deemed unfortunate in that the patient is weakened. A planet within 17 degrees of the Sun, either applying or separating, will still be subject to the weakening rays of the Sun.

Hayz (Haiz)
Hayz is defined by planets positioned either above or under the Earth, although authorities differ slightly in detail. Strength is given to:

> A masculine planet in a diurnal (day) chart, above the earth, in a masculine sign.
> A feminine planet in a nocturnal (night) chart, under the earth, in a feminine sign.

Masculine planets are the Sun, Mars, Jupiter, Saturn (and possibly Uranus and Pluto).
Feminine planets are the Moon and Venus (and possibly Neptune).
Mercury is flexible.
Masculine signs are Aries, Leo, Sagittarius, Gemini, Libra, Aquarius.
Feminine signs are Taurus, Virgo, Capricorn, Cancer, Scorpio, Pisces.

A diurnal planet (Sun, Saturn and Jupiter) is more dignified above the Earth in a day chart, and it seems that the nocturnal planets (Moon, Venus and Mars) are also more dignified above the Earth in a night chart.[14]

Reception
Planets in reception either by domicile or exaltation strengthens both planets. If the planets are in reception, initially in signs prejudicial to their intrinsic quality, this is likely to strengthen the constitution. For instance the Sun in Aquarius and Saturn in Leo, or Mars in Cancer and Jupiter in Capricorn. However it is much more advantageous to health if the original positions of the planets were in favourable signs, such as Mars in Leo and Sun in Aries.[15]

The greater number of testimonies of strength or weakness given to a planet is an indication of its mode of action in the chart. The following two chapters look at further factors that may affect the condition of the planet.

Revision
1. Which two areas of dignity are the strongest?
2. Name the two planets in rulership over the Earth triplicity.
3. How might the patient be described by planets in their detriment and fall?
4. If a planet is placed in a night sign, what might this indicate?
5. Explain peregrine.
6. In which house does Venus rejoice?
7. In which house does Saturn rejoice?

8. What might be suggested by a planet travelling faster than its mean motion?
9. What does William Lilly say about a stationary planet?
10. Which kind of planetary movement may create a change of temperature?

References
1. CA, p.104.
2. AG18, p.36.
3. ibid p. 28.
4. BI, p.261.
5. AG18, p.65.
6. ibid p.107.
7. ibid p.59.
8. CA, p.284.
9. AG18, p.59.
10. CA, p.284.
11. BI, p231.
12. AG18, p.59.
13. CA, p.258.
14. AG18, pp.13-14.
15. ibid p.41.

6

Fixed Stars and Azimene Degrees

When beggars die, there are no comets seen;
The heavens themselves blaze forth the death of princes.
            'Julius Caesar', Chapter 2, Scene 2. William Shakespeare

The Table of Dignities and Debilities shown in the last chapter is of prime importance in judging planetary strength, but additional information can be gained from monitoring the fixed stars and azimene degrees.

Fixed Stars

The fixed stars are so called because they appear almost motionless compared to the movement of the planets. Their motion is around 50 seconds per year, or in the region of one degree every 72 years. A planet, or angle, is in the field of influence of a fixed star when it is less than 2 degrees of orb by conjunction or opposition.

Fixed stars of the 1st magnitude are the brightest, and apparently most potent in human affairs. Yet Algol, of the 2nd magnitude, is often thought to be the most malefic fixed star, and it is suggested that this star casts its influence to an orb of 5 degrees either side of its position.[1] Regulus, of the 1st magnitude, is also thought to have an orb of 5 degrees.

The nature of fixed stars should be judged for their particular effects, though many do seem to be prejudicial to health. Fixed stars of a violent nature provide for some drastic change. Conjunctions to beneficial fixed stars apparently assist good health. It is possible that if the fixed star either conjuncts or opposes an angle or a planet already afflicted, the effects are more pronounced. Fixed stars of a malefic nature, if in conjunction or opposition to a significator in the chart, are not conducive to health. For instance:

> *A malevolent planet or violent Fixed Star, conjunct the ASC, extreme danger.* [2]

> *The Moon with the Pleiades and Aldebaran or with any other violent star, shows danger of death.* [3]

In view of the quote from William Shakespeare under the title heading, it would appear that fixed stars show up with more frequency in those decumbiture charts that come before the public in some way. It may, or may not, always be true. Given below is a list of fixed stars frequently considered. Further information can be sought from *The Fixed Stars and Constellations in Astrology* and *Fixed Stars and their Interpretation* by Vivian E. Robson, and *Brady's Book of Fixed Stars* by Bernadette Brady.

Signs	Fixed Star and Degree	Magnitude	Effect
Aries	Difda 2.44	2	Enforced change
Aries	Baten Kaitos 21.57	3	Falls, blows
Taurus	Mirach 0.27	2	Benefits
Taurus	Sharaton 3.58	3	Violence
Taurus	Hamal 7.40	2	Violence
Taurus	Algol 26.10	2	Power, violence
Taurus	Alcyone 29.59	2	Injuries
Gemini	Aldebaran 9.47	1	Integrity, but linked to illness
Gemini	Rigel 16.57	1	Benevolence
Gemini	Betelgeuze 28.45	1	Riches, also aggression
Cancer	Alhena 9.06	2	Wounds
Cancer	Sirius 14.12	1	Fame but linked to violence
Cancer	Wasat 18.31	3	Poison
Cancer	Castor 20.22	2	Distinction, also reversal of
Cancer	Pollux 23.13	1	Violence
Cancer	Procyon 25.47	1	Loyalty and friendship
Leo	Alphard 27.17	2	Drowning/poison
Leo	Adhafera 27.34	3	Acid/poison
Leo	Al Jabbah 27.54	3	Violence
Leo	Regulus 29.59	1	Courage and fortune
Virgo	Markeb 28.53	2	Injury turns to good
Libra	Vindemiatrix 9.56	3	Mourning, widow maker
Libra	Spica 23.58	1	Success and honours
Libra	Arcturus 24.22	1	Honour and prosperity
Scorpio	Acrux 12.00	1	Benefits

Scorpio	Agena 23.55	1	Refinement
Scorpio	Bungula 29.35	1	Honour and refinement
Sagittarius	Antares 9.46	1	Violence, bloodshed
Sagittarius	Rastaban 11.58	2	Violence, accidents
Sagittarius	Rasalhague 22.27	2	Depravity, perversion
Sagittarius	Sinistra 29.45	3	Poisoning
Capricorn	Spiculum 0.59	6	Eye problems, blindness
Capricorn	Ascella 13.47	3	Good fortune
Capricorn	Wega 15.27	1	Benefits, but linked to animal venom
Aquarius	Altair 1.54	1	Courage confidence
Aquarius	Dabih 4.03	3	Loss
Pisces	Fomalhaut 3.57	1	Wealth also maliciousness
Pisces	Deneb Adige 5.27	1	Generally favourable
Pisces	Markab 23.29	2	Violence
Pisces	Scheat 29.22	2	Murder/suicide

Azimene Degrees

If you see the Querent vitiated in some member…no doubt but you shall find the Moon, Lord of the Ascendant, or principal Lord of the Nativity or Question in one or more Azimene degrees. [4]
'Christian Astrology', William Lilly, p.118.

The quote above from William Lilly suggests that it is worth checking out a planet's condition for any link to an azimene degree. It seems that a planet, even in all its dignities, can be weakened if it happens to be conjunct one of these degrees.

Azimene degrees, also referred to as lame and deficient degrees, are as unfortunate as they sound. They occur in the following signs: Taurus, Cancer, Leo, Scorpio, Sagittarius, Capricorn and Aquarius. They are pertinent to all forms of astrology, horary, decumbiture and natal.

A planet found on one of those degrees usually points to a debilitating condition, a flaw or wound in part of the body, or problems with the senses, such as blindness or deafness. These degrees are given more weight if in conjunction to the Ascending degree, its planetary ruler, or the Moon. However, an important significator in conjunction with an azimene planet may also suffer in consequence, though it may not otherwise be debilitated.

In matters of ill health, the 6th house ruler is frequently connected to an azimene degree. Lilly does not demur in presenting a fearsome depiction of the azimene degree:

> *The ruler of sixth house afflicting square or opposition to ruler of Ascendant in Azimene Degrees, there will be no cure and the patient will suffer continual pain.*[5]

♈	-
♉	6 7 8 9 10
♊	-
♋	9 10 11 12 13 14 15
♌	18 27 28
♍	-
♎	-
♏	19 28
♐	1 7 8 18 19
♑	26 27 28 29
♒	18 19
♓	-

In the next chapter we will examine Azimene degrees and Fixed Stars in the chart of Natasha Richardson.

Revision
1. Where in the chart might the position of a fixed star do most damage?
2. In which kind of chart are fixed stars likely to show up with more frequency, those of ordinary individuals, or celebrities?
3. Name the fixed star which signifies 'contagious disease'.
4. Name one of the fixed stars linked to poison.
5. Which two aspects are the ones usually considered in placing fixed stars?
6. How are azimene degrees described?
7. How do azimene degrees affect the body?
8. In which position do azimene degrees do most damage?
9. Name the five signs in which azimene degrees do *not* occur.
10. In which sign do most of the azimene degrees occur?

References
1. CA, p.115.
2. ibid p.257.
3. ibid p.258.
4. ibid, p.118.
5. CA, p.250.

7

Antiscia, Arabic Parts and Midpoints

What wound did ever heal but by degrees?
'Othello', Act 2, Scene 3, William Shakespeare

Other factors worthy of consideration are antiscia, Arabic Parts and midpoints.

Antiscia

Antiscia, Arabic parts and midpoints share the common fact that they are calculated points in a chart, but the calculation is arrived at quite differently in each case. They may not be essential in a decumbiture chart, but they can indeed help in clarification or amplification.

The explanations may at first seem onerous but are quite easy to understand and calculate with practice.

Antiscia from the Greek meaning 'opposite shadows', refers to degrees mirrored across the solstice points. It is as if an imaginary line were to intersect between 0° Cancer and 0° Capricorn which resulted in both halves of the chart in mirror image to each other. For example, 1° of Cancer will mirror 29° of Gemini; 2° of Cancer will mirror 28° of Gemini, and so on. Antiscia are sometimes referred to as shadow or reflex points, and tie any planets placed on their opposite antiscia degrees into a relationship.

If two planets fall on each other's antiscium, this can be treated like a conjunction.[1] Antiscium degrees can be used in any type of chart under consideration. In decumbiture however, if Mars or Saturn are involved in an antiscium degree, this might worsen an already difficult situation, or blight a condition that initially looked promising. Naturally if Venus and Jupiter are involved in an antiscium degree, there may be help and protection forthcoming, but less so if the planets rule the 4th, 6th or 8th houses.

It is as well to mention the contra-antiscium. This is found as follows: if a planet is 3° Cancer, its antiscium will be 27° Gemini, and its contra-antiscium will be 27° Sagittarius. A planet positioned on the contra-antiscium may also add some useful knowledge to the matter at hand.

> *If both the lights are ill dignified and under the earth and in difficult aspect or Antiscium to Mars or Saturn, particularly if applying, this is testimony to a long illness.*[2]

Signs in Mirror Image to Each Other
Aries/Virgo
Taurus/Leo
Gemini/Cancer
Libra/Pisces
Scorpio/Aquarius
Sagittarius/Capricorn

Full Conversion Table of Antiscia

1 Can=29 Gem	1 Leo=29 Tau	1 Vir=29 Ar	1 Lib=29 Pi	1 Sco=29 Aqu	1 Sag=29 Cap
2 Can=28 Gem	2 Leo= 28 Tau	2 Vir=28 Ar	2 Lib=28 Pi	2 Sco=28 Aqu	2 Sag=28 Cap
3 Can=27 Gem	3 Leo=27 Tau	3 Vir=27 Ar	3 Lib=27 Pi	3 Sco=27 Aqu	3 Sag=27 Cap
4 Can=26 Gem	4 Leo=26 Tau	4 Vir=26 Ar	4 Lib-26 Pi	4 Sco=26 Aqu	4 Sag=26 Cap
5 Can=25 Gem	5 Leo=25 Tau	5 Vir=25 Ar	5 Lib=25 Pi	5 Sco=25 Aqu	5 Sag=25 Cap
6 Can=24 Gem	6 Leo=24 Tau	6 Vir=24 Ar	6 Lib=24 Pi	6 Sco=24 Aqu	6 Sag=24 Cap
7 Can=23 Gem	7 Leo=23 Tau	7 Vir=23 Ar	7 Lib=23 Pi	7 Sco=23 Aqu	7 Sag=23 Cap
8 Can= 22 Gem	8 Leo=22 Tau	8 Vir=22 Ar	8 Lib=22 Pi	8 Sco=22 Aqu	8 Sag=22 Cap
9 Can=21 Gem	9 Leo=21 Tau	9 Vir=21 Ar	9 Lib=21 Pi	9 Sco=21 Aqu	9 Sag=21 Cap
10 Can=20 Gem	10 Leo=20 Tau	10 Vir=20 Ar	10 Lib=20 Pi	10 Sco=20 Aqu	10 Sag=20 Cap
11 Can=19 Gem	11 Leo=19 Tau	11 Vir=19 Ar	11 Lib=19 Pi	11 Sco=19 Aqu	11 Sag=19 Cap
12 Can=18 Gem	12 Leo=18 Tau	12 Vir=18 Ar	12 Lib=18 Pi	12 Sco=18 Aqu	12 Sag=18 Cap
13 Can=17 Gem	13 Leo=17 Tau	13 Vir=17 Ar	13 Lib=17 Pi	13 Scor=17 Aqu	13 Sag=17 Cap
14 Can=16 Gem	14 Leo=16 Tau	14 Vir=16 Ar	14 Lib=16 Pi	14 Scor=16 Aqu	14 Sag=16 Cap
15 Can=15 Gem	15 Leo=15Tau	15 Vir=15 Ar	15 Lib=15 Pi	15 Scor=15 Aqu	15 Sag=15 Cap
16 Can=14 Gem	16 Leo=14 Tau	16 Vir=14 Ar	16 Lib=14 Pi	16 Scor=14 Aqu	16 Sag=14 Cap
17 Can=13 Gem	17 Leo=13 Tau	17 Vir=13 Ar	17 Lib=13 Pi	17 Scor=13 Aqu	17 Sag=13 Cap
18 Can=12 Gem	18 Leo=12 Tau	18 Vir=12 Ar	18 Lib=12 Pi	18 Scor=12 Aqu	18 Sag=12 Cap
19 Can=11 Gem	19 Leo=11 Tau	19 Vir=11 Ar	19 Lib=11 Pi	19 Scor=11 Aqu	19 Sag=11 Cap
20 Can=10 Gem	20 Leo=10 Tau	20 Vir=10 Ar	20 Lib=10 Pi	20 Scor=10 Aqu	20 Sag=10 Cap
21 Can=9 Gem	21 Leo=9 Tau	21 Vir=9 Ar	21 Lib=9 Pi	21 Scor=9 Aqu	21 Sag=9 Cap
22 Can=8 Gem	22 Leo=8 Tau	22 Vir=8 Ar	22 Lib=8 Pi	22 Scor=8 Aqu	22 Sag=8 Cap
23 Can=7 Gem	23 Leo=7 Tau	23 Vir=7 Ar	23 Lib=7 Pi	23 Scor=7 Aqu	23 Sag=7 Cap
24 Can=6 Gem	24 Leo=6 Tau	24 Vir=6 Ar	24 Lib=6 Pi	24 Scor=6 Aqu	24 Sag-6 Cap
25 Can=5 Gem	25 Leo=5 Tau	25 Vir=5 Ar	25 Lib=5 Pi	25 Scor=5 Aqu	25 Sag=5 Cap
26 Can=4 Gem	26 Leo=4 Tau	26 Vir=4 Ar	26 Lib=4 Pi	26 Scor=4 Aqu	26 Sag=4 Cap
27 Can=3 Gem	27 Leo=3 Tau	27 Vir=3 Ar	27 Lib=3 Pi	27 Scor=3 Aqu	27 Sag=3 Cap
28 Can=2 Gem	28 Leo=2 Tau	28 Vir=2 Ar	28 Lib=2 Pi	28 Scor=2 Aqu	28 Sag=2 Cap
29 Can=1 Gem	29 Leo=1 Tau	29 Vir=1 Ar	29 Lib=1 Pi	29 Scor=1 Aqu	29 Sag=1 Cap

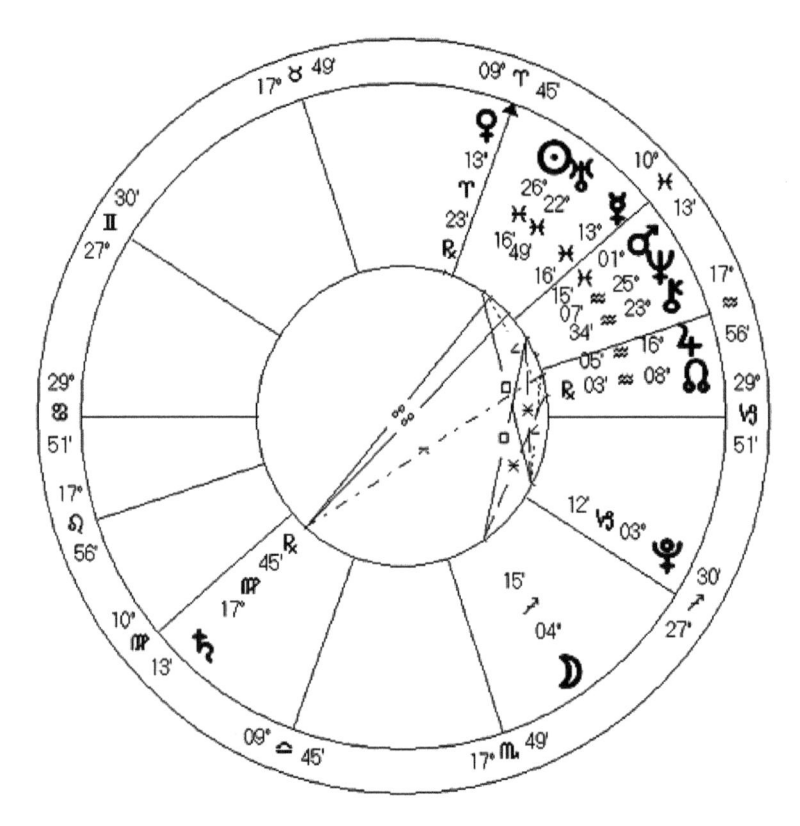

Example Decumbiture: Natasha Richardson, Fall
16 March 2009, 12:43 pm, Quebec, Canada. 46N49 071W14
Saturn 17° Virgo, Antiscion Venus 13° Aries

Natasha Richardson fell and received a blow to the head while taking a ski lesson. The planets subject to antiscium degrees are Venus and Saturn, which rule the 4th house of the grave and 8th house of death respectively. Note that both planets are retrograde and therefore virtually without movement.

Arabic Parts

The Arabic Parts (or Lots) are of ancient origin, but have come to be associated with Arabic astrologers when their works were translated into Latin. There are a great number of these parts or lots, though they are rarely used in modern astrology. The only part that seems to have survived the passage of time is that of the Part of Fortune. It may nevertheless be worthwhile to calculate the parts that are pertinent to the matter at hand, especially those pertaining to health or otherwise in a horary or a decumbiture chart.

The Part of Fortune, also referred to as *Pars Fortuna*, is a fortunate area in the chart promising health, wealth and happiness, unless spoilt by the rays of a malefic. It is calculated differently for a day-time chart (when the Sun is above the horizon) and a night-time chart (when the Sun is below the horizon). Some astrologers do not follow this rule, and they use the day time calculations for both day-time and night-time charts.

It is also customary to look at the strength/weakness of the dispositor of the Part of Fortune, which may well shed some light on the situation. (If the Part of Fortune is in Sagittarius the dispositor would be Jupiter, for instance.) This idea may also be applied to those parts that may be of use in a medical or decumbiture chart, though others may be considered too if they seem relevant in the particular matter at hand. These are principally:

Part of Fortune, Part of Sickness, Part of Death and Part of Fatality.

A planet or a point in the chart conjunct one of the parts, within a degree or so, will be influenced by that part, and it is possible that an opposition or square to the part may also be relevant.

Calculation of the Part of Fortune is based on the distance between the Sun and the Ascendant being equal to the distance of the Moon from the Part of Fortune in the same direction. A planet or an angle conjoining or opposing one of the parts will naturally come under its influence. It is also possible that a square aspect may apply.

The labour is naturally taken out of calculation by an astrological computer programme, which usually lists the many different parts. Ease of calculation by hand will be facilitated by turning the degrees and minutes of the points and planets into absolute longitude. Example given below.

Part of Fortune
    Day   ASC + Moon - Sun
    Night   ASC + Sun – Moon

Part of Sickness   ASC + Mars - Saturn

Part of Death   ASC + cusp of 8th – Moon

Part of Fatality   ASC + Saturn - Sun

Absolute Longitude (AL)

Absolute longitude translates degrees into the 360° of the zodiac circle and is used in many astrological calculations for simplification. The principle is as follows:

Aries, the start of the circle, becomes 0° in absolute longitude, thus 0 Aries. The next 30° relate to Taurus, the next 30° relate to Gemini, and so on. The following table sets this out clearly.

0° Aries starts at	0°	0° Libra starts at	180°
0° Taurus	30°	0° Scorpio	210°
0° Gemini	60°	0° Sagittarius	240°
0° Cancer	90°	0° Capricorn	270°
0° Leo	120°	0° Aquarius	300°
0° Virgo	150°	0° Pisces	330°

Example: Decumbiture chart for Natasha Richardson

Part of Fortune (Day chart)
    ASC 29°51' Cancer + AL 90°   = 119°51'
  + Moon 04°15' Sagittarius + AL 240° = <u>244°15'</u>
                                                    364°06'
  − Sun 26°16' Pisces + 330°   <u>356°16'</u>
                        Result   **07°50' Aries**

Part of Sickness
    Asc 29°51' Cancer + AL 90°   = 119°51'
  + Mars 01°15' Pisces + AL 330°   = <u>331°15'</u>
                                                    451°06'
  − Saturn 17°45' Virgo + AL 150°   <u>167°45'</u>
                        Result   283°21' − 270° AL
                                             = **13°21' Capricorn**

Part of Death
    Asc 29°51' Cancer +AL 90°   = 119°51'
  + cusp of 8th 17°56' Aquarius + AL 300° <u>317°56'</u>
                                                    437°47'
  − Moon 04°15' Sagittarius + AL 240° = 244°15'
                        Result   193°32' − 180°00' AL
                                             = **13°32' Libra**

Part of Fatality

Asc 29°51' Cancer + AL 90°	= 119°51'
+ Saturn 17°45' Virgo + AL 150°	= 167°45'
	287°36'
	+ 360°00
	= 647°36'
− Sun 26°16' Pisces + AL 330°	356°16'
Result	291°20' − 270°00' AL
	= **21°20' Capricorn**

Note: When the sum of the first two figures is smaller than the figure to be subtracted, add 360°. When calculations result in a figure higher than 360, one whole circle has been completed, so this amount is subtracted to find the equivalent zodiac degree. For instance 29° Aries is equivalent to 29° or 389° in absolute longitude since 389° − 360° = 29°.

In our example decumbiture for Natasha Richardson, the Part of Fortune at 7°50' Aries is a few degrees away from Venus, too wide to give any aid to the debilitated Venus. Any help would in any case be negated by the following factors:

> a) Dispositor of Aries, Mars, is in Pisces, which may be strong by triplicity, but placed in the 8th house of death, is ominous. It also has an afflicting square to the Moon.

> b) Further, the Part of Sickness 13°21' *Capricorn* and Part of Death 13°32' *Libra*, square and oppose Venus, effectively forming a 't'-square.

Midpoints

For those unaccustomed to using midpoints, they are defined by a planet (as well as the Ascendant, Midheaven or Node) placed at an equidistant point between two other planets. Calculation once again is facilitated by using absolute longitude. For example the midpoint between Saturn at 15° Taurus plus Neptune at 25° Taurus is 20° Taurus, i.e.

Saturn 15° Taurus	+	30°	=	45°00'
Neptune 25° Taurus	+	30°	=	55°00'
				100°00' divide by 2
				= 50° − AL 30°
				= **20° Taurus**

If Mercury were positioned at 20° Taurus, then it would be at the midpoint of Saturn/Neptune. This is called a direct midpoint. It is also possible for a planet to aspect a midpoint by opposition (180°), square (90°), half-square (45°) and sesquiquadrate (135°). These are called indirect midpoints but are just as effective in delineation.

The orb allowed is usually up to 1°30' degrees, so taking the above example, Mercury would be conjunct the Saturn/Neptune midpoint at 20° Taurus if it were at 18°30' degrees Taurus or 22°30' degrees Taurus. Though it is possible that the midpoint can still be effective up to 2° of orb.

There are four midpoints which are particularly associated with health conditions. These are as follows:

Midpoints
Mars/Saturn   Related to atrophy of an organ, or death
Mars/Uranus   Irregular rhythm of an organ, or accident
Mars/Neptune   Infection, paralysis of organism
Saturn/Neptune   Organic decomposition
Mars/Jupiter   Health

There may of course be other midpoints which can be taken into consideration if relevant.

The chart of Natasha Richardson has the beleaguered Venus on the midpoint of Mars/Neptune, i.e.

Mars 01°15' Pisces + AL 330°   =   331°15'
Neptune 25°07' Aquarius +AL 300° =   325°07'
                                      656°22' divide by two
                                  =   328°11' - AL 300
                                  =   **28°11' Aquarius**

Venus at 13°23' Aries is half-square (by 45°12') the Mars/Neptune midpoint at 28°11' Aquarius. In Natasha Richardson's chart this would probably refer to paralysis of the organism.

Venus, already essentially debilitated in the decumbiture chart, is further consigned to oblivion by the difficult effects of antiscia and Arabic Parts as well as the difficult midpoint. Venus in Aries rules the head and it was in this area of the body that the unfortunate Natasha Richardson received the fatal blow.

Incidentally, an azimene degree falls on the Descendant at 29° Capricorn, indicating that physicians were not in a position to help. The fixed star Markab at 23° Pisces is conjunct Uranus, which highlights the accidental aspect of the tragedy. A fuller analysis of the decumbiture chart relating to NR is covered in Chapter 22.

Revision
1. Between which two degrees and which two signs is the antiscium line drawn which results in both halves of the chart in mirror image to each other?
2. When would Venus or Jupiter involved in an antiscium degree not be as helpful as they would normally be?
3. What is the antiscion of 14° Libra?
4. What is the Arabic Part in most common usage, and how is it calculated in a day chart?
5. At which degree of absolute longitude does Sagittarius begin?
6. How is the Part of Sickness calculated?
7. Define a midpoint.
8. Which is commonly referred to as the 'illness midpoint'?
9. What is the orb commonly allowed to a midpoint?
10. Which midpoint is associated with death?

References
1. HAR, p.143.
2. CA, p.258.

8

Aspects

These late eclipses in the sun and moon portend no good to us.
'King Lear', Act 1, Scene 2, William Shakespeare

The angular relationship between the planets, or aspects, form the basis of delineation. The harmonious aspects [sextile (60°), trine (120°)] usually connect signs of similar or congruent element. For example Fire to Fire, or Fire to Air. In a medical sense these aspects allow physiological functions to run smoothly. In effect, they help to maintain homeostasis.

The square (90°) and opposition (180°), the so-called inharmonious aspects, connect signs of discordant nature. This may create problems mentally or physiologically as well as possible organ congestion. The conjunction (0°) is harmonious or difficult depending upon the planets involved. Aspects across dissociate signs, even if termed harmonious, may create a slightly more discordant energy.

Whilst the traditional aspects above are of initial importance in judging a chart, it may be a mistake to overlook other aspects, especially the inconjunct (150°), which may indicate weakened organ function. Or put another way, may indicate weak transmission of vital spirits between certain organs/tissues of the body. Problems may also arise with the half-square (45°) or sesquiquadrate (135°). These latter aspects may not be conducive to maintaining homeostasis.

The trine of an inherently benefic planet is more fortunate than the trine of a malefic. The square of a malefic is more harmful than that of a benefic.[1] It seems however, that the more benefic the planet, the less harm will its square inflict. Or if a planet is malefic and in detriment or a difficult house, its trine aspect may also cause difficulties.[2]

Applying aspects are more powerful than separating ones, for good or ill. Also sinister aspects (following the direction of the signs) are more powerful than dexter aspects.[3]

In the principle interpretation of decumbiture charts (as well as horary charts), the main emphasis is on the traditional aspects (conjunction, sextile, square, trine and opposition) between the traditional planets (Moon, Mercury, Venus, Sun, Mars, Jupiter, Saturn), possibly due to the following reasons:

1) The outer planets (Uranus, Neptune and Pluto) were not discovered when these astrological rules were laid down.

2) The outer planets are thought to influence global or group events; this may be epidemics, or plagues, or in some circumstances where the person's fate is carried along with others. It might however be worthwhile to consider outer planets if they appear to be relevant to judgement.

3) Traditional planets ostensibly deal with earthly matters, or physiological systems. In decumbiture we are enquiring about the physical body; outer planets may deal with more ethereal matters, like the subtle bodies (see chapter on Subtle Bodies). However, when involved with traditional planets, outer planets may indeed affect physiological systems.

Aspect Orbs
Modern astrology gives the orb allowable to a particular aspect. However, this is not the case in traditional astrology; it is the planet that designates the orb. Computer charts will use the orb allowed for an aspect, so it would be advisable to check aspects in accordance with the table below.

The Moieties of the Orbs of Planets According to William Lilly [4]

	Orb	Moon	Mercury	Venus	Mars	Jupiter	Saturn
Sun	17	14.75	12	12.5	12.25	14.5	13.5
Moon	12.5	-	9.75	10.25	10	12.25	11.25
Mercury	7	9.75	-	7.5	7.25	9.5	8.5
Venus	8	10.25	7.5	-	7.75	10	9
Mars	7.5	10	7.25	7.75	-	9.75	8.75
Jupiter	12	12.25	9.5	10	9.75	-	11
Saturn	10	11.25	8.5	9	8.75	11	-

As can be seen, each planet has a designated orb. For instance, the Sun has 17, the Moon 12.5. Added together that equals 29.5. Divided by 2 the answer is 14.75. This means that any aspect between the Sun and Moon has a moiety of 14.75. Moiety refers to half the diameter (the radius) of the orb of influence. The orb is a sphere of influence with the planet at its centre. So if the Sun is 5° Aries and the Moon is 19° Aries, they are technically still in conjunction. It is possible however that the wider the moiety the less strong is the aspect.

Perfection
Various movements of the planets can sometimes prevent the aspects from perfecting, that is becoming exact, which may prolong the illness, or affect it in some way. These are:

Prohibition
If two planets are applying to one another but another planet intercepts before the original aspect can be completed, this usually prevents an event from happening, for better or for worse. For example, Venus at 5° Libra may be trying to effect a conjunction with Mars at 10° Libra but before she can do so, Mercury (a faster moving planet) at 9° Capricorn perfects a square with Mars.

Frustration
This is similar to prohibition in that a planet, for instance Mercury at 5° Libra, is trying to reach the conjunction of Venus at 10° Libra, but before this aspect can be affected Venus completes a square with Saturn at 11° Capricorn.

Refranation
Two planets may be applying to one another but before they can perfect an aspect, one of them turns retrograde. Alternatively, the planet receiving the aspect from the faster moving planet actually moves into the next sign before perfection of the aspect can take place.

Order of Speed of the Planets
Moon, Mercury, Venus, Sun, Mars, Jupiter, Saturn

Revision
1. What might be said to be the basis of chart delineation?
2. What is the difference between modern and traditional methods of designating the orb of an aspect?
3. How do the traditional harmonious aspects help to maintain health?
4. What possible effect do the traditional inharmonious aspects have on the body?
5. Name the traditional planets in order of speed.
6. What other aspects might also be considered in delineation?
7. How might the outer planets manifest in health?
8. What moiety of orb exists between Jupiter and Saturn?

9. If Mercury is at 5 degrees Scorpio and Venus at 11 Scorpio, would they still be in conjunction?
10. With which planet has Mercury the greatest moiety of orb?

References
1. AG, p.73.
2. ibid p.75.
3. ibid p.80.
4. CA, p.107.

9

The Constitution

The First House

It is the stars, the stars above us, govern our conditions.
'King Lear', Chapter 4, Scene 3, William Shakespeare

Examination of the 1st house in terms of strength and weakness of the constitution is always the first consideration. This may reflect the constitution as designated in the nativity though not always. Quite often, the 1st house will also point to the part of the body under affliction.

Of great significance is the comparison in strength of the 1st house, in terms of the Ascendant ruler and planets positioned therein, to the 6th house ruler, and planets in the 6th house.

The stronger the Ascendant and its ruler, the better it is for the individual in terms of quick and easy recuperation. Wherever there are afflictions, intervening aspects from the two Fortunes (Venus and Jupiter), may ameliorate a difficult situation, especially if the Fortunes are stronger than the Infortunes (Mars and Saturn).

It is an art therefore, in judging the strength of the planets, especially when there are contradicting factors, as is often the case. Few planets are completely free of some debility, whether from sign or house position, aspects, antiscia, midpoints or other cosmic factors. The 1st house may be judged as follows:

a) Zodiac sign ascending
b) Aspects from planets to the ascending degree
c) The planetary ruler of the first house
d) Planets positioned in the first house

a) Sign Ascending

Fire and Air signs have always been deemed stronger than Earth and Water signs, but this is only one point of consideration and may mean little when other factors are taken into consideration. The rising sign or Ascendant may give an indication of the area or part of the body under examination, though not always. If planets are positioned in the following sign to the rising sign but in the 1st house, this may complicate the condition, or indicate another area of the body under affliction, should the planets be in debility.

In horary charts, the ascending first three degrees and the last three degrees of a sign usually declare that the chart cannot be judged, as it is either 'too early' or 'too late', and if judgement were to go ahead, a wrong answer may result. However, early or late degrees in a decumbiture chart often suggest that the condition is in its early or late stages respectively, for good or ill, depending on ruling planetary strength or debility, and other factors in the chart. A horary chart signifies only a possibility, since it is the horoscope of a question, whereas the decumbiture chart usually describes an event.

b) Aspects to the ascending degree

The planet which is conjunct, square or in opposition to the Ascendant, as well as the Ascendant ruler, could signify the disease. Aspects to the ascending degree from malefic planets are likely to be detrimental to health, but more so if the aspect is a difficult one. If a benefic planet is in good aspect to the Ascendant this could ameliorate threats from elsewhere.

c) Ruler of Ascendant

Good Health

In order for the life force to flow unimpeded, the planetary ruler of the Ascendant should ideally be well placed by sign and humour. This might be in domicile or exaltation, or in a compatible humour. In the latter situation, a contradiction occurs in some instances where the mode of action is the same but the planet finds itself in debility, as in the cold and moist Venus in the cold and moist Scorpio, where it is in detriment. This suggests that the consistency of the life force may be at variance.

In an ideal situation, the Ascendant ruler would also be placed in an amicable house, at least not in a cadent house, which is traditionally weak; though contradictions occur once again since the Sun has its joy in the cadent 9th house and the Moon in the cadent 3rd house. Rather than allowing such contradictions to confuse, it is advisable to include them in the general judgement of strength. Recuperation may at times move slowly, perhaps, intermittently.

To continue the thread of superlative health, the Ascendant ruler should receive beneficial aspect from the rulers of the 5th, 9th or 11th houses, preferably from a Fortune. Certainly there should be no aspects from the rulers of the 6th or 8th houses, nor the 12th. And should neither the rulers of the 6th and 8th houses aspect the Moon and Sun, good health is more or less assured.[1]

The Ascendant ruler must also avoid aspects from Mars or Saturn (and the same for the Sun and Moon) for hope of improvement.[2] Yet all hope is not lost even if the Ascendant ruler should be afflicted, if the Fortunes throw a beneficial aspect its way.[3] It's always more helpful if the Fortune is stronger than the afflicting Infortune however.

There are rare cases where the ruler of the Ascendant receives no aspects whatsoever, so it may be judged that the vital spirits, or life force, is at a standstill, nothing moving either way. This of course is not likely to aid quick recovery. There may be a protracted wait before the ruler is involved in an aspect, or moves into another sign or house, which will advance the condition either way.

Culpeper is quite optimistic and decrees that if the ruler of the Ascendant is debilitated by sign or house, and enters into another sign or house, provided it is not the 6th, 8th or 12th, the disease ends in health.[4]

Bad Health

Adverse aspects to the Ascendant and its ruler are probable, since, after all, a decumbiture chart is one relating to a health condition. Weakness is initially ascertained by noting if the Ascendant ruler is in debility by sign, house and aspect.

The Ascendant ruler in detriment or fall tends to weaken the constitution, and discomfort is apparent if it is in a sign contrary to its intrinsic humour. For instance, a hot and dry planet like Mars would be uncomfortable in a cold and dry sign like Virgo, yet perhaps not so bad if placed in Capricorn, also cold and dry, but where the planet is exalted. If the ascendant ruler is in terms of a malevolent planet (Mars and Saturn) this weakens it. (See the Table of Dignities and Debilities.) A difficult situation arises if the Ascendant ruler receives aspects from Saturn or Mars.

The Ascendant ruler placed in difficult houses such as the 6th, 8th and 12th indicates problems, depending on sign and aspects of course. Or if it receives a difficult aspect from the rulers of those houses.[5]

An Infortune afflicting the ruler of the Ascendant, from the 8th house, is particularly difficult.[6] Indeed if the Ascendant ruler is on cusp of the 8th house, it is not a good omen, and no blessings are heaped upon it if it is in the 7th house either, since it then opposes the ascendant (life).[7]

Whatever the condition the Ascendant ruler, the Moon should be considered in judgement too since it also represents the patient as well as monitoring the progress of the condition or disease. An afflicted Ascendant ruler with an afflicted Moon does not help matters.[8] The patient will get worse if the Moon applies by bad aspect to the ruler of the Ascendant. If the Moon opposes the ruler of the Ascendant in an afflicted condition such as being retrograde or combust, the condition is not easily curable.[9]

Yet the Moon can come to the rescue if it is strong and applies to the Ascendant ruler with a trine or sextile, since it can ameliorate a difficult situation.[10] The good it does is negated if the Moon rules the 8th house.[11]

Not forgetting of course, that if the Fortunes cast beneficial aspects to the significators, this can also ameliorate a dire situation. If the ruler of the Ascendant is weak, but joined to a Fortune, there will be recovery.[12]

Comparison with Sixth House Ruler
A very important consideration is the comparison between the Ascendant ruler and the planetary ruler of the 6th house. If, after reflection on dignities and debilities, house position, aspects etc., the Ascendant ruler proves stronger, then it can be assumed that the patient has the vigour to withstand the disease and overcome his condition. That is the general rule. However, if the planetary ruler of the 6th house is stronger, then a struggle ensues to overcome the illness.

In some charts the planet ruling the Ascendant and that of the 6th house are of equal strength, which may suggest a fluctuating situation or a tug or war. Sometimes the disease or condition is stronger, at other times the patient seems to be on the mend. For further consideration, judge the aspects from other planets to both the ruler of the Ascendant and 6th house. If the ruler of the Ascendant is weaker than the planet afflicting it, this further weakens the patient.[13]

For further comparison of the two rulers, it might be helpful to consider the aspects to the 6th house cusp, as one would to the Ascendant degree.

d) Planets in the First House
Determine the strength of planets placed in the 1st house. A Fortune placed therein strengthens the constitution as opposed to an Infortune, which weakens it. Good planets in the Ascendant and midheaven strongly maintain life, purportedly.[14] Such may be the Sun, Jupiter, Venus or the Moon, preferably not afflicted by a difficult aspect from the rulers of the 6th or 8th houses or by Mars or Saturn. The stronger the Fortune, the better the situation.

A long disease threatens if the ruler of the 6th house is placed in the 1st house and that of the 1st house placed in the sixth.[15]

If Mars or Saturn applies to a planet in the 1st house, health difficulties are indicated and recovery likely to be protracted. With an Infortune in the Ascendant, something changes,[16] no doubt for the worse. But such a pronouncement should not be taken at face value, since Saturn has joy in the 1st house, and if dignified may not cause great affliction. Yet should it rule one of the malefic houses, and the Ascendant ruler is poorly dignified, its strength may work against the patient, after all.

It appears that an afflicted Moon placed in the 1st house, particularly by the ruler of the 8th or Saturn, does not help the patient. The Moon in the 1st house can be particularly difficult because she has more power over the body.[17] The situation may be ameliorated if the Moon is in reception with the afflicting planet apparently.[18]

Further Considerations
Regarding the Ascendant Ruler

There is a further consideration in judging the Ascendant ruler. In the normal scheme of things, the Ascendant ruler positioned in a certain sign will point to the part of the body ruled by that sign. However, in the scheme outlined in the following table, there is a variation.

A planet positioned in the sign that it rules, will rule the head. For instance, the Sun in Leo rules the head; if the Sun is in the next sign, Virgo, the throat is highlighted, followed by the shoulders in Libra, the heart in Scorpio, and so on down the body to the feet. Or at least, that is the theory.

Each planet when positioned in the sign that it rules will therefore rule the head, in the second sign from his own, it will rule the throat, in the third sign from his own, the shoulders, and so on. Consult the Table to understand this more clearly. This presumably gives a further indication of the part of the body under affliction.

It is also worth examining this table in relation to the 6th house ruler. Though there is a danger that this judgement may become more complicated, it is also possible that repetition of a particular organ or area of the body by this means, may be helpful in pinpointing the part under affliction.

What Members in Man's Body Every Planet Signifieth in any of the Twelve Signes[19] (Members in Man's Body)

	Saturn	Jupiter	Mars	Sun	Venus	Mercury	Moon
Aries	Breast Arms	Neck Throat Heart Belly	Head Belly	Thighs	Kidneys Feet	Genitals Legs	Knees Head
Taurus	Heart Breast Belly	Shoulders Arms Belly Neck	Kidneys Throat	Knees	Head Genitals	Thighs Feet	Legs Throat
Gemini	Belly Heart	Breast Kidneys Genitals	Genitals Arms Breast	Legs Ankles	Thighs Throat	Head Knees	Feet Shoulders Arms Thighs
Cancer	Kidneys Belly Genitals	Heart Genitals Thighs	Feet	Knees Shoulders Arms	Knees Shoulders Arms	Legs Throat Eyes	Head Breast Stomach
Leo	Genitals Kidneys	Belly Thighs Knees	Knees Heart Belly	Head	Legs Breast Heart	Feet Arms Shoulders Throat	Throat Stomach Heart
Virgo	Thighs Genitals Feet	Kidneys Knees	Legs Belly	Throat	Feet Stomach Heart Belly	Head Breast Heart	Arms Shoulders Bowels
Libra	Knees Thighs	Genitals Legs Head Eyes	Feet Kidneys Genitals	Shoulders Arms	Head Intestines	Throat Heart Stomach Belly	Breast Kidneys Heart Belly
Scorpio	Knees Legs	Thighs Feet	Head Genitals Arms Thighs	Breast Heart	Throat Kidneys Genitals	Shoulders Armes Bowels Back	Stomach Heart Genitals Belly
Sagittarius	Legs Feet	Head Knees Thighs	Throat Thighs Hands Feet	Heart Belly	Shoulders Arms Genitals Thighs	Breast Kidneys Heart Genitals	Bowels Thighs Back
Capricorn	Head Feet	Legs Neck Eyes Knees	Arms Shoulders Knees Legs	Belly Back	Breast Heart Thighs	Stomach Heart Genitals	Kidneys Knees Thighs
Aquarius	Head Neck	Feet Arms Shoulders Breast	Breast Legs Heart	Kidneys Genitals	Heart Knees	Bowels Thighs Heart	Genitals Legs Ankles
Pisces	Arms Shoulders Neck	Head Breast Heart	Heart Feet Belly Ankles	Genitals Thighs	Belly Legs Neck Throat	Kidneys Knees Genitals Thighs	Thighs Feet

Revision
1. Why is it of crucial importance to examine the 1st house?
2. What might the last few degrees on the Ascendant suggest?
3. Which type of house (Angular, Fixed, Cadent) might be the weakest for the placement of the Ascendant ruler?
4. Aspects from which planets might seriously debilitate the Ascendant ruler?
5. Why might the Ascendant ruler be debilitated in the 7th house?
6. If the Ascendant ruler is stronger than the 6th house ruler what might this suggest?
7. Aspects from the rulers of which three houses could be detrimental to the Ascendant ruler?
8. Whatever condition the Ascendant ruler may be, the Moon should also be considered in judgement. For what reason?
9. What effect would a Fortune have being placed in the 1st house?
10. Which malefic has joy in the 1st house?

References
1. AJD, p.26.
2. ibid p.104.
3. ibid p101.
4. ibid p.100.
5. ibid p.100.
6. CA, pp.256-7.
7. AJD, p.100.
8. CA, p.253.
9. ibid p.258.
10. ibid p.255.
11. AJD, p.103.
12. ibid p.101.
13. CA, p.251.
14. AJD, p.105.
15. ibid p.99.
16. ibid p.107.
17. ibid p.108.
18. CA, p.253.
19. ibid p.119.

10

Illness

The Sixth House

The miserable have no other medicine, but only hope.
'Measure for Measure', Act 3, Scene 1, William Shakespeare

The 6th house represents the illness, or its outward symptoms. It is an unfortunate house because it has no traditional aspect to the Ascendant. The 6th house should be judged in the same way as the 1st house, namely:

    a) The sign on the cusp
    b) The planetary ruler
    c) Planets placed therein.

a) Sign on 6th house cusp

Note the sign on the sixth cusp. It may suggest the part of the body under affliction. The *element* to which the sign belongs may also be indicative of the *humour* which may be out of balance.

Fire represents the choleric humour and tends to overheat the body, suggesting inflammation. Earth, the melancholic humour, could indicate a condition which stems from depression or some hardening in the body; Air, the sanguine humour, can indicate a blood disease, and wind, stemming from indigestible substances. Water, the phlegmatic humour, suggests too much mucous in the body, as well as oedema, disturbance of water balance. (See chapter on the Four Humours.)

The *quadruplicities* indicate the current progress of the condition, its general behaviour and how far advanced it may be. Cardinal signs (Aries, Cancer, Libra, Capricorn) suggest that the condition may have only just begun, but may be moving rapidly ahead for good or ill. Fixed signs (Taurus, Leo, Scorpio, Aquarius) imply that the condition could be well be entrenched and not moving quickly for good or ill. Mutable signs (Gemini, Virgo, Sagittarius, Pisces) suggest that the condition fluctuates in severity, often prolonging it.

If there is an intercepted sign within the 6th house, especially if planets are placed therein, the condition may be obscured. Something within the organism may be malfunctioning but there is difficulty in determination.

It might be helpful to check for close aspects from any of the planets, whether good or ill, to the cusp of the 6th house.

How far advanced and area of body
The number of degrees on the 6th house cusp tend to show the stage the condition has reached. Early degrees (0 to 10) of the sign on the cusp hint at its beginning; the middle (10-20) indicates the disease is well on its way. The last degrees (20-30) suggest the disease is culminating, and heralds a change in the condition.[1]

Where in the body
In general, masculine signs govern the right side of the body, and feminine signs the left.

Right side of body
If the ruler of the 6th house is afflicted above the earth (7-12 houses), and in a diurnal sign (day sign), the sickness is in the right side of the body, and in the upper part of it, from the stomach to the head.[2]

Left side of body
If the ruler of the 6th or significator of the disease is in a feminine sign and in aspect to a feminine planet, the disease is in the left side of the body.[3]

If the significator is in few degrees of the sign, the upper part of the body is under affliction, the middle of the sign corresponds to the middle of the body, and the last degrees of the sign, the lower part of the body.

Planetary ruler of 6th house
The strength of 6th ruler should be compared to that of the 1st house ruler. If judged stronger, then the disease is stronger than the patient, and the patient needs to be strengthened by the right remedies. Far better for the ruler of the Ascendant to be stronger than the ruler of the 6th house, as this infers greater ability to fight the disease.

If the planets ruling the Ascendant and the 6th house appear to be approximately equal in strength, this might indicate that sometimes it is the illness which dominates, at other times the patient's constitution has the ascendancy.

Particular note should be made of the planet/s and place from which the ruler of the 6th last separated and the next planet to which it applies.

There is good indication of recovery if the planetary ruler of the 6th separates from a malefic (Mars or Saturn) and applies with a sextile or trine to a benefic, no matter how bad things look apparently. It is not so beneficial the other way round!

An afflicted 6th house ruler indicates a difficult and possibly protracted illness, especially if afflicted by a strong 8th house ruler, or 4th and 12th house ruler.[4] The same can be said for difficult aspects between the 6th house ruler and Mars, Saturn as well as the Moon and Sun.

If the ruler of the 6th house is in the 1st house, and vice versa, the condition is likely to continue until one of the planets moves out of the sign or house.[5] View any connection between the 6th house ruler and the 1st as suspect, especially if the ruler of the 6th applies to the ruler of the 1st by square or opposition. The disease in that case is increasing and is not yet at its height or full growth.

Planets in the 6th house

Surprisingly perhaps, the 6th house ruler in the 6th house indicates a swift cure, if it is a Fortune and strongly dignified. It is obviously not so fortunate if the 6th house ruler and that of the 8th are in each other's houses, a situation not conducive to easy recovery unless there is a good aspect between them.

The Moon apparently disturbs the functions of the body quite severely in the 6th house, especially if afflicted by the rulers of the 1st, 6th or 8th houses.[6] It appears however, that if the Moon is unafflicted it could spell just a short illness. If the Moon is in a difficult aspect with Venus, the affliction may be due to overindulgence. Venus may also point to gynaecological problems. Nevertheless if Venus or Jupiter is in the 6th, and unafflicted, there is stronger possibility of cure.

The Infortunes, Mars or Saturn, and severely afflicted positioned in the 6th, threaten a dangerous disease.[7] More so if there are challenging aspect to the rulers of the 1st, 4th, 6th, 8th or 12th houses. Or indeed, if the rulers of one of the aforesaid houses are in the 6th house.

Should one of the Fortunes be placed in the 6th house along with an Infortune, this might be a protective influence.[8] Any malefic planet in the 6th house or any planet peregrine and unfortunate in that house, is indicative of disease.[9] Neither is it a good sign if the South Node is in the 6th house.[10]

Questions
1. Why is the 6th house unfortunate, according to William Lilly?
2. Why is the 6th house ruler compared in strength to that of the Ascendant ruler?
3. How do the mutable signs on the 6th house cusp describe a condition?
4. What do early degrees on the 6th house cusp indicate?
5. Which house rulers imply difficulties if in aspect to the ruler of the 6th house?
6. If there is a Fortune and Infortune in the sixth, what might this imply?
7. State two indications of good recovery.
8. What might it signify if the ruler of the 6th is moving out of one sign to another?
9. If the ruler of the 6th house is afflicted above the earth (7-12 houses), in which side of the body might the illness be, right or left?
10. Which side of the body might the disease be found if the ruler of the 6th is in a feminine sign and in aspect to a feminine planet?

References
1. CA, p.264.
2. ibid p.263-4.
3. ibid p.263.
4. AJD, p.68.
5. CA, p.250.
6. EMA, p.547.
7. AJD, p.99.
8. CA, p.248.
9. ibid p.258.
10. ibid p.289.

11

The Physician

The physician must be able to tell the antecedents, know the present, and foretell the future - must mediate these things, and have two special objects in view with regard to disease, namely, to do good or to do no harm.
'Epidemics', *Hippocrates*, Book 1, Chapter 2,
translated by Francis Adams

The Planetary Hour
It appears that the nature of the meeting between physician and patient can be determined by the planetary hour. Apparently, the disease is likely to be a cold one if a physician first visits a patient in the hour of Saturn, and in any case a cure is unlikely (supposedly!). The hour of Mars brings a hot condition, but no matter what the physician does, the patient is unlikely to be grateful![1] Is it possible however, that should the Infortunes be dignified, this could ameliorate the outcome?

Naturally the situation improves greatly if physician and patient meet in the hours of Jupiter or Venus, so much so that, whether the physician cures the patient or not, he/she shall nevertheless be looked upon favourably.

But whether a Fortune or Infortune, if the planetary hour is badly afflicted – combustion being the most calamitous – the patient may be in a very sorry state.[2]

The planetary hour begins at sunrise which needs to be checked in the ephemeris on any particular day. The first hour will accord with that of the planet ruling the day, as follows:

Sunday – Sun
Monday – Moon
Tuesday – Mars
Wednesday – Mercury
Thursday – Jupiter
Friday – Venus
Saturday – Saturn

The 7th house

Good connections between the patient and physician are recommended since not only is recovery a question of choosing the right medication but also the right kind of spiritual and psychological help. Culpeper said:

> *Many a times I find my patients disturbed by trouble of conscience and sorrow and I have to act the divine before I can be physician. In fact our greatest skills lies in the infusion of hopes, to induce confidence and peace of mind.*[3]

The cosmic indications relating to the 7th house will describe a physician or healer that can help or hinder the progress of his patient.[4] Quite simply, if the planetary ruler of the 7th house is strong and without affliction, there is likelihood that the physician will cure the patient, or at least offer some help.

Contrariwise, if the planet ruling the 7th house is weak and afflicted, there is likelihood that the physician will not cure the patient, or even be able to help.

An Infortune positioned in the 7th house augers a 'paltry physician'. Culpeper is quite decided on the matter.[5] Saturn in the 7th may suggest the wrong diagnosis or very little rapport existing between patient and physician. Mars here might indicate a physician who is too rash in his pronouncements, or the South Node, which brings coolness,[6] chilling the relationship between physician and patient. Presumably the North Node helps to establish warmer relations.

Should the ruler of Ascendant be in the 7th house opposing the Ascendant this is deemed unfavourable.[7] This is particularly so if the planet is in its fall, afflicted by the Infortunes or confronting the presence of the ruler of the 8th in the 7th house. If the same planet rules both the 7th and 8th, it is certainly not very auspicious for a resounding cure, or if the ruler of the 8th is in the 7th house.[8] The ruler of the Ascendant in 7th may also show someone who endeavours to be his own physician, efficacy of which most probably depends on planetary strength and lack of affliction.

Venus or Jupiter in the 7th house will of course indicate a physician that is deemed helpful, but as always careful examination of the planet/s is necessary if that premise is to be fulfilled. Debilitated planets, albeit Fortunes, do not always have the strength to carry out their promise.

The following quote from Lilly suggests that for a physician and his medicines to be really effective, the condition of the 10th house should be examined.

> *The 7th house represents the Physician, the 10th house his medicine. If the Lord of the 7th be unfortunate, the Physician shall not cure. If the 10th house or Lord thereof be unfortunate, his physick is improper.*[9]

Questions
1. How does the planetary ruler of the 7th house show the likelihood of the physician being able to aid the patient?
2. If the 10th house ruler should be afflicted but the 7th house ruler dignified, how might this affect the physician's ability to help?
3. If the ruler of the Ascendant is in the 7th, opposing the Ascendant, is this conducive to self-medication?
4. How is the patient likely to act if the patient is seen in the hour of Mars?
5. In which state should the planetary ruler of the 7th be in order to effect a cure?

References
1. CA, pp.256-282.
2. ibid p.283.
3. Dylan Warren-Davis quoting from O. Thulesius 'Nicholas Culpeper, English physician and astrologer', The Macmillan Press Ltd 1992, *The Traditional Astrologer*, Issue 7, 1994.
4. CA, p.282.
5. AJD, p.72.
6. BI, p.233.
7. AJD, p.100.
8. CA, p.257.
9. ibid p.282.

12

The Terminal Triangle

The Fourth, Eighth and Twelfth Houses

The Terminal Triangle – the 4th, 8th and 12th houses – refers to the end of life; each house with a subtle difference. The 4th house may describe the conditions at the end of life, as well as old age, and the grave. The 8th has no affinity with the Ascendant, and therefore, with Life. The 8th also refers to the liberation of the soul, and it is possible that difficulties in this area suggest death as a happy release after much suffering. The 12th house has no affinity with the Ascendant, and it is also described as the imprisonment of the soul, bringing day to day restriction, mental or physical.

End of the Matter
The Fourth House

Any man's death diminishes me, because I am involved in mankinde.
John Donne 'Devotions'.

The 4th house refers to the end of the matter, or how the illness terminates in terms of speed as well as suffering. Since the 4th is also referred to as the grave, it can indicate the demise of the patient.

> *The 4th house signifies the end of the sickness, and whether it will terminate quickly, or endure long. Fixed signs prolong, common (mutable) signes vary the disease, moveable (Cardinal) ones shew an end one way or other quickly.*[1]

A Fortune in the 4th house indicates a good and speedy end to the illness, unless it is the ruler of the 8th house. The Infortunes in the 4th house may suggest that the time before health is restored will be lengthy. Or that the patient is heading towards his final resting place, with supporting evidence of course. The most pertinent aspects from the ruler of the 4th house are to the rulers of the 1st, 6th and 8th houses: Life, Sickness and Death respectively. It's preferable that there are none! If the planetary ruler of the Ascendant is positioned in the 4th house, this may be a warning of impending difficulties. This is more likely if it is debilitated and afflicted by the Infortunes.[2] However, supporting evidence is necessary for the worst outcome, such as the Moon afflicting the ruler of the 8th house or the ruler of the 8th house in the 10th house.[3] Aspects between the 4th and 6th are usually unhelpful, especially when the 6th house ruler is positioned in the 4th. This can suggest a grievous illness.[4]

Likewise, the rulers of the 4th and 8th in difficult aspect, particularly the conjunction, threaten a difficult illness.[5] If the rulers of the Ascendant and 8th house meet up in a conjunction in the 4th house it creates a dire situation, this being the house of the grave.[6] If the ruler of the 4th house is an Infortune and applies to the ruler of the 8th house, this can signify a dangerous situation.

Crisis and Death
The Eighth House

It is unwise to prophesy either death or recovery in acute diseases
Aphorisms, 'Hippocratic Writings', Ed. G.E.R. Lloyd, p.210.

The 8th house, not to mince words, signifies death, and whilst a difficult cosmic picture could indicate the demise of the patient, this need not be the only interpretation. Other possibilities include organ congestion, fracture of limbs, wounds or surgery. The eighth house also indicates poisoning, and the effect of drugs on the body.[7] It is also a house of worry, for as Lilly says, it brings *"fear and anguish of Minde"*.[8] Crisis of some kind is indeed a feature of this house. Nevertheless, even if the situation looks grim, it would be unethical to pronounce the worst. Hopefully the ruler of the 8th house is placed in some innocuous place in the chart, and does not influence the judgement. Nevertheless, the 8th house ruler's aspects should be considered in terms of malevolence or otherwise. It is important not to jump to alarming conclusions. Dr Edward Bach, the founder of the Bach Flower remedies, was told that he only had about three months to live after a stomach operation for cancer. He lived another twenty years or so. A baby (Jamie Ogg) born to a mother in Australia on 25 March 2010 was pronounced dead on delivery but showed signs of life two hours later.

8th House and Ascendant
As long as the planetary ruler of the 8th house does not afflict the Sun, Moon and ruler of the Ascendant, there is hope that the patient will recover quickly. In a decumbiture, however, it is not often that all three points are in such a good cosmic position, but they would all have to be severely afflicted before the worst can be thought, if not pronounced. The strength of the

Ascendant ruler against that of the 8th house ruler should be considered. If the 8th house ruler is stronger than that of the Ascendant ruler, this may indicate a hard battle to regain health.[9] For instance, with the ruler of the 8th house in an angular house, and the ruler of the Ascendant in a cadent house, the latter would be deemed weaker, at least by house position. This spells danger to the patient apparently, particularly if an Infortune is in an angular house. Or indeed if the ruler of the 8th house is positioned in the 1st house.[10] In the same way, severe affliction of the Ascendant ruler if positioned in the 8th house, threatens a severe illness. These indications may be threatening but naturally other evidence needs to be considered, such as strength and dignity of the Moon, the Sun and the two Fortunes.

Indications of adverse consequences occur if the Ascendant ruler and that of the 8th house are involved in a difficult aspect with each other such as the conjunction, square or opposition.[11] Even if the 1st and 8th houses are connected by aspect or reception, there is hope of recovery if the malefic planets are not involved, and if the planets are Fortunes.[12] Or if there should be a sextile or trine from Jupiter to planets involving the 1st and 8th houses, this can ameliorate the condition. In the same way, a sextile or trine from Venus or Jupiter to the Ascendant or ruler of the 6th house, or to the Moon, may lessen the difficulty. If the planetary ruler of the Ascendant disposes that of the 8th, there is more hope of recovery than the other way round. Is it not better that life dispose of death then that death dispose of life?[13]

8th House and the 6th House
If the rulers of the 6th and 8th are in each other's houses, with an aspect between them, the situation is dire, unless the aspect is a sextile or trine.[14] It is less severe also if neither planet is afflicted by an Infortune. If the same planet rules the 6th and 8th houses, this is a dire warning that the illness may end in death, depending always on supporting factors. A dire situation arises if planets in the 6th and 8th houses are in difficult aspect to each other, or their rulers.[15]

The 8th House and the Moon
A strong and unafflicted Moon may support life despite difficult considerations in the chart. But if the Moon applies by aspect to a planet in the 8th, this does not bode well for health.[16] A debilitated Moon placed in the 8th house weakens the patient especially combustion.[17] As always, particular attention is paid to the planet from which the Moon separates or departs by aspect, and its condition. The Moon transferring the light and influence of the ruler of the Ascendant to the ruler of the 8th hints at death, especially when the ruler of the 8th is in the Ascendant, the ruler of the Ascendant

and the Moon being both afflicted.[18] A dire position might include the ruler of the 8th house, retrograde and conjunct, square or opposing the Moon.[19] If the ruler of the Ascendant is in reception with the planet in the 8th, death can be avoided, though the illness may be severe and long.[20]

Hospital and Restriction
The Twelfth House

The very first requirement in a hospital (is) that it should do the sick no harm.
Florence Nightingale, 'Preface to Notes on Hospitals'
(1859, 3rd Ed. 1863)

Significators in the 12th house indicate confinement both physical and mental. The patient may not be able to influence his circumstances, or he may be confined in a hospital or other place of restriction. Problems linked to the above may result when the ruler of the Ascendant is in difficult aspect with the ruler of the 12th house.

> *The lord of the Ascendant in bad configuration of the lord of the sixth or twelfth shows little hopes of recovery.* [21]

But this needs to be substantiated by other factors in the chart. For instance, should the ruler of the 6th as well as the Moon be involved in a configuration with the 12th house, this does indeed worsen the situation.[22] Since the 12th house may also indicate mental problems, there is possibility of confinement. At one time this might have been in a mental asylum. Witchcraft was assigned to the 12th house, and illness, particularly mental illness was once thought to have been the result of a spell. Certainly the balance of the mind may be suspect if a planet in the 12th house is in difficult aspect with Mars, but this is particularly the case if that planet rules the Ascendant or the sign in which the Moon is placed.[23]

For further corroboration of mental illness the condition of Mercury and the Moon should be considered. The 'self-undoing' aspect of the twelfth house may be apparent if the ruler of the 6th house is in the 12th, since the patient may be responsible for his own condition.[24] If the physician/healer is working closely with his patient and notes the movement of the planets over the ensuing days, it is as well to note if the ruler of the Ascendant moves into the 12th house (or for that matter the 6th or 8th house) since this can be detrimental to health. Naturally, if the ruler of the Ascendant moves into a good house, an angular house for instance, there may be improvement.

Revision
1. Besides death, what other interpretations are given to the 8th house?
2. If a Fortune is in the 4th house, how might the illness terminate?
3. Which would be stronger, at least by house position: the ruler of the 1st house in an angular house, or the ruler of the 8th in a cadent house?
4. If the Infortunes are placed in the 4th house, would the duration of illness likely be long or short?
5. If the rulers of the 8th and 6th are in each others houses, and in aspect, what would lessen the severity of the illness?
6. Why is an illness severe if the ruler of the 8th house makes a difficult aspect to the Moon?
7. What is the best possible indication of recovery?
8. Which house refers to the grave?
9. Why should the strengths of the Ascendant ruler and that of the 8th house ruler be examined?
10. If the ruler of the 6th house is positioned in the 12th house, what might this signify?

References
1. CA p.282.
2. ibid p.257.
3. ibid p.257.
4. AJD p.98.
5. CA p.284.
6. ibid p.256.
7. BI, p.275.
8. CA p.54.
9. ibid p.283.
10. AJD p.105.
11. CA p.257.
12. AJD p.104.
13. ibid p.105
14. CA p.250.
15. EMA p.424.
16. CA p.256.
17. ibid p.258.
18. ibid p.256-7.
19. ibid p. 257.
20. ibid p. 257.
21. ibid p.258.
22. ibid p.251.
23. ibid p.265.
24. AJD p. 98.

13

Physic

The Tenth House

I swear by Apollo the healer, by Aesculapius, by Health and all the powers of healing, and call to witness all the gods and goddesses that I may keep this Oath and Promise to the best of my ability and judgement.
'Introduction to Hippocratic Oath', *Hippocratic Writings*, edited by G.E.R. Lloyd, p.67

The Rules

Physic or medicine is largely ruled by the 10th house, its planetary ruler and planets therein.[1] The best indication of a successful cure is if the 10th house ruler is a Fortune – Venus or Jupiter – and in good aspect to the ruler of the Ascendant, or the Moon. In any event, the strength of the 10th house ruler, whichever planet it may be, has to be considered.

It would seem however, that if the 10th house ruler is afflicted, the wrong medicine might be used, or the medicines are of no help. This is confirmed when a weak 10th house ruler also afflicts the ruler of the Ascendant or the Moon. It might be advisable to send the patient to another practitioner, especially if the condition is a serious one.

However, there may be ameliorating factors in the chart that show some benefit may still be gained in the current consultation. For instance, if there are Fortunes situated in the 10th house, without affliction. Even a Fortune in the first house might be suggestive of helpful medicine.

If good planets be in the Ascendant or Midheaven at Decumbiture and pretty strong withal, they will stand to their tackling stoutly to maintain life, though the significators of it be never so much afflicted. [2]

Yet if the planet in the 10th rules the 8th house, it is certainly not conducive to a cure, especially if afflicting the Ascendant ruler. In that case *"the physitian will be in a shrewd mistake, and instead of curing go near to kill."* [3]

The Application of Physic

The decumbiture chart shows which herbs should be used. The sign on the 10th house cusp, its ruler, aspects and any planets in the 10th house would give some indication of choice.

Naturally, the planet/s ruling medicine would have to be unafflicted. If the astrologer is a herbalist or aromatherapist, plants within the Materia Medica and their associated planets might be selected. Since there are often several plants under planetary rulership it is incumbent upon the practitioner/astrologer to determine which constitutes the best physic.

Culpeper also gives the following indications in determining illness and choosing medications.[4] It may well be that rather than following the rules slavishly, they should be taken more as guidelines.

The Way of mixing Medicines according to the cause of the disease, and part of the body afflicted

1. Fortify the body with herbs of the nature of the Lord of the Ascendant, whether a Fortune or Infortune: Jupiter and Venus, Mars and Saturn respectively.

This will strengthen the patient's vitality.

2. Let the remedy be something antipathetical to the Lord of the 6th.

In other words, chose medicines that are opposite in nature to the 6th house ruler. For instance, if cold Saturn rules the 6th, then herbs that are warm may be helpful.

3. Let the remedy be something of the nature of the sign Ascending.

Choose medicines that are positively of the nature of the Ascendant.

4. If the Lord of the 10th be strong, make use of his medicines.

Healing occurs if medicines are chosen that are of the nature of the Lord of the 10th house, providing planet is dignified.

5. If the Lord of the 10th is weak, make use of the medicines of the Light of Time.

The Sun by day, above the horizon; the Moon by night, below the horizon.

6. Be sure always to fortify the grieved part of the body by sympathetical remedies.

Choose medicines that are in harmony with the ailing part of the body. For instance, ailments of the liver may respond well to Jupiter remedies.

7. Always regard the heart, because the Sun is the fountain of life.

Choose remedies ruled by the Sun, usually of a cordial nature.

Favourable Moment for Physic

It was thought that the body would more readily respond to treatment if propitious times for medication were chosen. Similarly, medicines might also be changed from time to time in accordance with the condition of the patient, and the planets. This might safeguard against a build up of toxicity, as well as be a precaution against the patient becoming too accustomed to the medicine which may prove less effective.

Medications might be increased when the Moon waxes in light, from New Moon to Full Moon (conjunction to opposition), or the medicines can be decreased when the Moon decreases in light, from Full Moon to New Moon (opposition to conjunction).

The Moon's passage through the sign or signs as well as aspects to the planets might be observed for a favourable moment for dispensing medicines to attain a certain effect. Culpeper calls these the Four Administering Virtues: Attractive, Digestive, Retentive and Expulsive.[5]

> Fire signs governed the *Attractive Virtue* responsible for the heat and energy of the body.
> Air signs governed the *Digestive Virtue* and kept the digestion in order.
> Earth signs governed the *Retentive Virtue* when patient needed to keep from expelling food.
> The Water signs governed the *Expulsive Virtue* to allow free flowing of liquids such as menstruation or oedema.

Planetary Hours

To take the administration of herbs to a finite point, planetary hours might be considered. It appears that when treating a part of the body or its function, the corresponding planetary hour to the appropriate physiology would be most efficacious. If dealing with gynaecological problems – the Procreative Virtue – Culpeper suggests the following:

> *Observe the hour and medicines of Venus, to fortify; of Mars to cleanse this virtue of Saturn to extinguish it. Therefore medicines ruled by Venus should be given in the Planetary hour ruled by Venus, if the aim is to fortify or invigorate the area. If the aim is to purge or cleanse the procreative area, plants ruled by Mars might be more appropriate in a Mars ruled hour, or those of Saturn 'to extinguish it' in a Saturn ruled hour.*[6]

To invigorate the procreative area, a choice from Venus-ruled plants or oils might be *Rose* with its reputation for regulating the menstrual cycle and aiding fertility. Or perhaps *Geranium*, reputedly a hormone balancer.

To purge and cleanse the procreative area, a choice from the Mars-ruled plants or oils might be *Vitex (Agnus Castus)*. A hot plant therefore could be efficacious in purging and cleansing and regulating reproduction. In this regard it is easier to see why this plant has been given Mars rulership (despite its strong link to the womb). Another Mars-ruled plant or oil could be *Pine* with its cleansing action on the uterus, as well as the urinary and digestive systems. In the normal scheme of things it is not a plant/oil one would initially think of using in matters of reproduction, but following the idea of planetary hours and virtues, it seems to make some sense.

To 'extinguish it' referring to the reproductive system, might relate to the menopause, since that is when the menstrual cycle is 'extinguished'. There is a Saturn-ruled plant/oil that is very well known for its efficacy in this regard, and that is *Cypress*. It's strongly astringent quality halts excess, such as hot flushes, perspiration, heavy menstruation as well as oedema. Another plant/oil may be *Tea Tree*, although it does not have a traditional planetary rulership, but its sudorific properties may be helpful in excessive perspiration.

The *vital virtue* is ruled by the Sun which is linked to the blood circulation, and the vital spirits. Strengthening the heart would be in the hour of the Sun, according to this scheme, and one of the best tonics for the circulatory system ruled by the Sun is *Lemon*. It is said to stimulate the white corpuscles and invigorates the immune system aiding the body to fight infectious disease. *Rosemary* also Sun ruled, is valuable as a heart tonic and apparently a cardiac stimulant as well as normalising low blood pressure.

The *natural virtue* is given to Jupiter, associated with the liver. "*Its office is to nourish the body and is dispersed through the body by the veins.*"[7] It is possible that Culpeper is actually referring to the arteries which 'nourish the body' by carrying oxygen and nutrients to the tissues of the body. *Linden Blossom*, ruled by Jupiter, apparently has a detoxifying effect on the liver, as well as diuretic effect on the kidneys. *Melissa* in the Jupiter group has a tonic effect on the liver and spleen. It is also known as a blood cleanser, as well as calming the heart rate.

Medicines for the brain might be given in either the hours ruled by the Moon or Mercury. Mercury governs the rational part of the brain while the Moon governs sensation.[8] Therefore, take herbs of Mercury to invigorate the brain in the Mercury hour, such as marjorma, and Moon herbs perhaps to calm the nerves in the Moon hour, such as clary sage.

Saturn herbs in the Saturn hour improve the memory, apparently. The Mars hour would presumably help to energise the body with Martian herbs. Saturn tends to block the influence of the Sun, and Mars exacerbates the heat of the Sun. The Infortunes respective actions could create a situation describing low and high blood pressure respectively.

The above are only guidelines and other plants, herbs and oils may be more appropriate depending upon individual circumstances. A list of plants/oils and their planetary rulership, traditional and conjectural, follows in Chapter 17 as well as contra-indications and precautions.

Revision
1. What is the best indication of a successful cure?
2. What might indicate in the chart that the wrong medicine had been used?
3. If the ruler of the 10th house is weak, how else could one discern which medicines to use?
4. What does Culpeper say if a planet positioned in the 10th rules the 8th house, especially if afflicting the Ascendant ruler?
5. Which planet is the 'fountain of life'?
6. Describe the path of the waxing Moon.
7. When might be a good time to decrease medicines?
8. What temperature is accorded to Mercury herbs?
9. If the aim is to correct a fluid imbalance in the body, in which element would it be preferable for the Moon to be placed in?
10. How might the body be affected at the Full Moon?

References
1. CA p.282.
2. AJD, p.105.
3. ibid.
4. CH, p.210-11.
5. ibid pp.214-5.
6. ibid p.212.
7. ibid p.213-13.
8. ibid.

14

The Humours

He (the physician) knew the case of everich maladye,
Were it of hoot or cold, or moiste, or drye,
And where engendred, and of what humour;
He was a verrey parfit practisour.
The physician in Chaucer's 'Canterbury Tales'

The concept of the four humours as a model of the universe is thought to have originated in ancient Egypt or Mesopotamia. Greek physicians and philosophers subsequently adopted this idea around 400 BC.

It was thought that the four humours arose from unity, or wholeness, or light. The primary quality of light is heat. Heat radiates on matter, which is the absence of heat, namely cold. Between the two is humidity, the opposite is dryness. The four humours are subsumed in the fifth element, ether.[1]

Anaximander c.610-c.545 BC, a Greek philosopher of the Ionian school, proposed that the origin of the universe resulted from the separation of opposites from primeval matter: hot, cold, dry and wet. It was thought that heat and cold had an effect on the production of all four humours in the body. [2]

The Greek physician Hippocrates (c.460-377) known as 'the father of medicine' is credited with disseminating the humoural theory, which remained the bedrock of medicine for at least two thousand years. The human body, thought to be composed of the four basic humours, was deemed healthy when the state of these constituent substances was in the correct proportion to each other in strength and quantity. Whenever this balance was disturbed, ill health resulted.[3]

The word 'humour' derives from the Latin humor meaning fluid, which refers to blood, bile and lymph. Physicians understood this to refer to the composition of the blood and the efficient, or otherwise, transportation of fluids within it. By examining the humours, or the fluids, principally blood, the strength of the vital force or spirits circulating throughout the body could be judged.

Mercury represents the vital force, or perhaps more accurately the flow of the vital force, since it was the planet of ideas, which influenced emotional attitudes and physiological function. Ether could either flow like a liquid or act like a gaseous vapour. It was also referred to aqua vitae or the water of life.[4]

Ether also represented the consciousness that united the four humours linked to the four elements as well as all human sensory impressions. Galen, c.129 AD, a Greek physician who practised in Rome, developed the doctrine of the temperaments based on Hippocrates' humoural theory. Temperament, from the Latin temperare or 'mix and mingle', refers to the way mind and will function in an individual. Therefore the basic temperament of an individual was sourced from his or her humoural composition.

The humours, elements and temperaments were all related. When the flow of the vital force within the body was disturbed, usually through an imbalance of the four humours, health was affected, though it could be restored usually through plant medicine and often in accordance with the planets. Each humour was symbolised by a planet, its strength or weakness in the horoscope related to the health of the body.

An individual's dominant temperament or humour suggested certain behaviour characteristics principally in the nativity, as well as in the decumbiture though perhaps of a more temporary nature. The decumbiture chart through its planetary and house placements may reveal the current offending humour. Each of the humours was also affiliated to an element: Fire, Earth, Air and Water. Vettius Valens was the earliest astrologer to assign elements to the triplicities.[5]

The sanguine humour is the principal humour of the blood, and embodies the other three humours: the choleric, melancholic and the phlegmatic. The sanguine humour allied to the Air element rules over the general constitution of the blood. The choleric humour, linked to Fire, refers to the circulation of the blood; the phlegmatic humour – Water – is the blood plasma, the fluid medium of the blood largely consisting of water in which the blood cells circulate. Melancholic – Earth – refers to the sediment of the blood or plasma proteins that contribute to the blood's viscosity.

The staunch and rational qualities of the sanguine and melancholic types were generally preferred over the emotional phlegmatic and excitable choleric types. Feeling and self-assertion were not encouraged it seems, and indeed actively repressed. William Lilly in his tome *Christian Astrology* gives a method by which one's predisposing temperament can be determined in the natal chart.[6]

The following table gives a correlation between the zodiac signs and the humours.[7]

Humours: Zodiac Signs

Zodiac Sign	Gender	Nature/Humour	Elements	Quadruplicity
♈	Masculine	Hot & Dry Choleric	Fire	Cardinal
♉	Feminine	Cold & Dry Melancholic	Earth	Fixed
♊	Masculine	Hot & Moist Sanguine	Air	Mutable
♋	Feminine	Cold & Moist Phlegmatic	Water	Cardinal
♌	Masculine	Hot & Dry Choleric	Fire	Fixed
♍	Feminine	Cold & Dry Melancholic	Earth	Mutable
♎	Masculine	Hot & Moist Sanguine	Air	Cardinal
♏	Feminine	Cold & Moist Phlegmatic	Water	Fixed
♐	Masculine	Hot & Dry Choleric	Fire	Mutable
♑	Feminine	Cold & Dry Melancholic	Earth	Cardinal
♒	Masculine	Hot & Moist Sanguine	Air	Fixed
♓	Feminine	Cold & Moist Phlegmatic	Water	Mutable

Humours: Planets

Element	Humour	Seats	Planetary Ruler	Nature
Earth	Melancholic (Black Bile)	Spleen	♄	Cold & Dry
Water	Phlegmatic (Phlegm)	Lungs	♀	Cold & Moist
Ether	Vital Force	Heart	☿	
Fire	Choleric (Yellow Bile)	Gall	♂ ☉	Hot & Dry
Air	Sanguine (Blood)	Liver	♃	Hot & Moist

Mercury represents the flow of the vital force, but could align itself to any of the humours depending upon sign and closest aspect.

Planetary heat and cold derives from the planets' relationship with the Sun, which is the source of heat and light and the Earth which is the source of moisture. The Moon lacks the warmth of the Sun and is cool and moist; Saturn is cold and dry because it is furthest from the warmth of the sun and the moisture of the earth.

The sanguine humour links to the **Air** signs, and rules the composition of the blood and the quality of transportation of respiratory gases and nutrients to the tissues. This humour might suggest corrupted or putrefied blood, even leprosy, and hand and foot gout.

The sanguine humour has its seat in the liver, ruled by Jupiter
The liver is the largest of the internal organs and has many functions but basically it regulates the main chemicals in the blood, as well as help clear the bloodstream of toxic substances.

The melancholic humour links to the **Earth** signs, referring to blood viscosity (depth of thickness) with the possibility of a sluggish blood flow. Depression could be a symptom. It seems that tuberculosis was linked to the melancholic humour. Any fever present would be long lasting.

The melancholic humour has its seat in the spleen, ruled by Saturn
The spleen's main function is to produce lymphocytes (red blood cells) and act as a reservoir for red blood cells for use in emergencies. Its secondary function is to break out worn-out, non-functioning red and white blood cells and blood platelets.

The phlegmatic humour links to the **Water** signs, and rules over fluids such as the lymph, sweat, urine, cerebro-spinal fluid, blood plasma and synovial fluids of the body. The phlegmatic humour, indicated illness that stemmed from moist conditions which might indicate coughs, or stomach ailments.

The phlegmatic humour has its seat in the lungs ruled by the Moon and Venus
The main purpose of the lungs is to supply the body with oxygen for cell metabolism, as well as to eliminate carbon dioxide, the waste product. Each lung is enclosed in a double membrane called the pleura, allowing the lungs to slide freely as they expand and contract during breathing.

The choleric humour links to the **Fire** signs, and corresponds to the blood cells, especially the erythrocytes and the body's production of heat and energy. The choleric humour might indicate the blood boiling over, fevers and anger.

The choleric humour has its seat in the gall, ruled by the Sun and Mars
The gall is another name for bile, a thick, bitter, greenish-brown fluid formed from waste products in the liver. It consists of water, mucus, bile pigments such as bilirubin, cholesterol and various salts. Bile leaves the liver through the bile ducts and is stored in the gallbladder. Thereafter it is discharged into the small intestines to help digest and absorb food, particularly fats.

Chart Delineation in terms of Humours

As can be seen from the above, the signs and planets are classified by their degrees of hot, cold, dry and wet. Venus for instance is cold and moist and when placed in a cold and moist sign like Pisces, is not only acting in accordance with its intrinsic quality, it emphasises a particular humour. Whilst it may ostensibly indicate a state of humoural balance, aspects to Venus could suggest otherwise. For instance, a difficult aspect from Jupiter may exacerbate the particular humour in question, or one from Saturn may restrict the humour. This could unbalance the phlegmatic humour as represented by Venus in relation to the fluids of the lymphatic system, ruled by Pisces, either by expansion or contraction respectively. The result may either be oedema of the feet, or dry skin, to suggest an example.

The planets generally cast their influence in terms of heat or moisture to planets receiving them by applying aspect. For instance, Saturn cools and dries to the extreme, Jupiter gives moderate heat, and Mars gives extreme heat and dryness. The Sun also heats and dries but heats more than Mars. Venus is cold and moist but tending towards moisture, whereas Mercury is cold and dry but tending towards dryness. However, like the Moon, Mercury is easily influenced by other planets. The Moon is cold and moist, but at different times of its cycle it can be increased in moisture and heat. It tends towards warmth with increasing light and to cold with decreasing light.[8]

The significator of the querent, or patient, in a sign contrary to his own nature, as for example Mars naturally hot and dry in Cancer which is cold and moist, indicates discomfort or sickness.[9] Planets placed in signs against their degree of hot and cold and not in sympathy with the planet function less efficiently, and so does the patient.[10]

The 6th house may show the offending humour at the time of the decumbiture. This however, may only be one indication. Perhaps the sign on the 6th house cusp, the ruler's sign position and the planets positioned in the 6th house, should also be considered. Not least, the sign position of the Ascendant ruler must also be taken into account, and comparisons made.

In a healthy person the humours remain in a state of balance, allowing the life force to flow freely through the body, and are not distinguishable.[11] Should a humour be found to be out of balance, it is well to consider the seat of the humour in terms of the organ it represents. This may or may not be a pointer to the underlying condition. Ultimately, using the humours in judgement of the decumbiture, may only act as reinforcement to delineation.

Revision
1. Which Greek physician is credited in introducing the concept of the four humours?
2. Which principle fluid of the body does the word 'humour' refer to?
3. Which planet rules ether, representing the consciousness that united the four humours or four elements as well as all human sensory impressions?
4. Which elements belong to each of the four humours?
5. Which humour might be prone to pessimism, depression and constipation, and the blood clotting mechanism of the blood?
6. Which humour might give illnesses connected to oedema?
7. In which part of the body is the sanguine humour said to have its seat?
8. In which part of the body is the choleric humour said to have its seat?
9. With which humour is Aquarius associated?
10. Which humour and element is cold and moist?

References

1. Zoller R. *Lost Key to Prediction*, Inner Traditions International Ltd, 1980, pp.36-7.
2. CM, p.66.
3. *Hippocratic Writings*, Translated by J. Chadwick and W.N. Mann, Penguin Classics 1950, p.26.
4. Warren-Davis D. The articles on 'Introduction to Decumbiture' in The *Traditional Astrologer*, various issues.
5. Gieseler Greenbaum, Dorian. *Temperament: Astrology's Forgotten Key*, The Wessex Astrologer, 2005, p.21.
6. CA, p.532.
7. Abu Mashar, *The Abbreviation of the Introduction to Astrology*, trans. Burnett, Arhat, 1997, pp.2-3.
8. BI, p.232.
9. AJD, p.37.
10. ibid.
11. Warren-Davis D. 'Introduction to Decumbiture', *The Traditional Astrologer*, Issue 2, 1993.

15

Timing and Length of Disease

*The course of 'acute' diseases, especially, is determined by 'critical days', when marked changes take place in the patient' symptoms and this doctrine of critical days must be recognised as one of the main motives for carrying out and recording **daily** observations.*
'Hippocratic Writing', edited G.E.R. Lloyd, p.32

General Considerations

Various factors are taken into account regarding length of illness, including the time of year, apparently. Falling sick in autumn or winter threatens a long illness, whereas a speedier recovery is probable if sickness begins in spring or summer.

Timing with regard to zodiac signs[1]
Cardinal or moveable signs (Aries, Cancer, Libra, Capricorn) suggest conditions that are acute or swift in duration. Days are indicated.
Fixed signs (Taurus Leo, Scorpio, Aquarius) take firm hold of disease, and have therefore a possibility of long and deep-seated conditions lasting months, possibly leading to years.
Mutable or common signs (Gemini, Virgo, Sagittarius, Pisces) are changeable, coming and going, returning just when the situation is thought safe. So they might lengthen sickness with the possibility of weeks and months.

The Ascendant
Considerations regarding length of illness in connection with the Ascendant according to Culpeper and Lilly include:[2]

a) A quick end to the illness if the Ascendant ruler is fast in motion and is going from one sign to another, or one house to another, as long as it is not the 6th or 12th house.
b) Ascendant ruler slow in motion, illness slow in parting.
c) If the ruler of the Ascendant receives an applying aspect from the ruler of the 6th house by square or opposition, the disease is still increasing and is not yet at his height or full growth.

d) If the Ascendant ruler, Sun or Moon are in aspect to Mars or Saturn, this tends to prolong the disease.

e) If the ruler of the Ascendant is in the 6th house and vice versa, the disease will be long and continue until one of the planets moves out of the sign. If the next aspect is square or in opposition to the ruler of the 4th or 8th, or to Saturn or Mars, and they are slow in motion, a long illness is signified.

f) Judging the time the patient recovers may be accomplished by observing the aspect of a benevolent planet to the ruler of the Ascendant. Check how many degrees there are distant between them, in what house they are in – angular, succedent or cadent – and what signs they are in – cardinal, fixed or mutable.

Sixth House

The degree/s on the 6th house cusp hint at the length of the illness. Early degrees of the sign show the beginning of illness, and late degrees that the illness is coming to an end for better or worse. If the last degree is on the 6th house cusp, then something will change in the condition when the sign changes.[3] This also applies to a planet going from one sign to another.

If there is a intercepted sign in the 6th house, something has come to a halt, there is no development in either direction, good or bad. Whether the illness might be counted in days, weeks, months or years depends upon whether cardinal, fixed or mutable signs are on the house cusp, and supported by other factors in the chart. Fixed signs on the sixth house cusp may not necessarily indicate years, rather that the illness is hard to shift.

Planets in the 6th house supplement other factors regarding length of disease. It appears that when a Fortune is in the 6th and unafflicted, and not the source of disease, the disease will not be permanent.[4] However, if an infortunate planet is in the 6th, and is removing out of one sign into another, the disease will speedily alter, perhaps even for the better.

If the planet in the 6th house rules the Ascendant, and the 6th house ruler is in the first house,[5] the disease is likely to be long and will continue until one of the planets moves out of the sign. If the next aspect is square or in opposition to the ruler of the 4th or 8th, or to Saturn or Mars, and they in are slow in motion, then the situation looks quite grave.

The Moon is inconstant but action depends upon sign, house and aspects. If the Moon is in a fixed sign it indicates a longer illness than if it were in a cardinal sign, which tends to be quick acting. In a mutable or double-bodied sign, the length of the disease is likely to be unpredictable. An applying Moon to the Ascendant with a difficult aspect means the illness worsens, and will increase in length if the Moon is slow in motion. If the Moon is swift in motion, the cure comes more quickly.[6]

Mercury is also inconstant but likewise everything depends upon the aspects it makes. A retrograde Mercury weakens the life force and prolongs the condition.

Venus gives neither a long disease nor a short one, but middling,[7] which gives hope of recovery but uncertainty of length. Though generally Venus is indicative of a short illness. But as usual other factors such as strength need to be taken into consideration, as well as benefic or malefic aspects.

The Sun brings short, hot diseases.[8] If the Sun as well as the Moon and the ruler of the Ascendant are unafflicted, and apply with good aspect to the Fortunes, then the cure comes quickly. The Sun and Moon afflicted by Saturn in angles may cause "*a tedious long llness*". [9]

Mars also brings short diseases with quick resolution but may be acute.[10] Mars may intensify the illness especially if applying to a square of Jupiter.

Jupiter tends to bring short diseases.

Saturn lengthens any disease and produces chronic infirmities resulting from depression.[11] If slow in motion, in a fixed sign, as well as retrograde, it lengthens the disease still further. An ameliorating factor is if Saturn is in a cardinal sign and in any of his terms or swift in motion.

Note: Overall, it seems that the Infortunes, Mars and Saturn, particularly when placed or ruling the 6th house, prolong disease. If Saturn is placed in an angle (1st, 4th, 7th, 10th), and afflicts both the Sun and Moon, there is likelihood of a long disease.

The 6th house ruler applying by difficult aspect to the Ascendant ruler could intensify the illness and prolong it. Generally speaking the disease may be a lengthy one if the ruler (or planets in the 6th house) are combust, retrograde, slow in motion, or in their detriment or fall. Or if the 6th house ruler is placed in the 8th house and is square, conjunct or opposing Mars or Saturn.

Monitoring Disease

Acute or Chronic Disease
Acute or short-lived sickness is judged by the transit of the Moon. Its progress throughout the signs and houses describes the development of the illness, and the likely termination for good or ill.

If the illness does not terminate by the time the Moon returns to the same place as it was at the time of the decumbiture (about a month), then this is judged a chronic disease and is then monitored by the movement of the Sun.[12]

Following the course of the Moon and Sun may assist the therapist/physician/healer in changing or altering the treatment.

Crisis Days involving the Moon

The word 'crisis' derives from the Greek word to judge or discern, whether good or bad.

The *first* critical day involving the transit of the Moon, depending upon its speed, will be around seven days from the decumbiture, at which time the Moon will be square to its original place. The *second* critical day, will be around the fourteenth day at the opposition of the transit Moon to the decumbiture Moon. The *third* critical day would be anticipated on the twentieth or twenty-second day, being the second square of the transit Moon to the decumbiture Moon, with the *fourth* critical day occurring around the twenty-eighth day, depending upon the speed of the Moon. The transit Moon would then conjunct its original place. For example:

>*Decumbiture* Moon 4 June 2012　　　　　　　14°43' Sag
>Tr. Moon 10 June 2012 (first critical day)　　14°43' Pisces (sq)
>Tr. Moon 18 June 2012 (second critical day)　14°43' Gem (opp)
>Tr. Moon 25 June 2012 (third critical day)　　14°43' Virgo (square)
>Tr. Moon 1 July 2012 (fourth critical day)　　14°43' Sag (conj)

Critical days may indicate a crucial turn in the condition, though it is often useful to monitor the Moon's aspects in between the designated critical days. Indeed, Lilly suggests that the 45 degree and 135 degree aspects to its decumbiture place should also be monitored: the transit of the Moon within three and ten days respectively.[13]

The following Aphorisms by William Lilly and Nicholas Culpeper may aid judgement.[14]

Moon's transits to Decumbiture

- If the Moon is in dignity on a critical day, the situation looks hopeful (the reverse if in debility).

- The condition of the Moon on a critical day should be noted with regard to the meeting with the Fortunes, or Infortunes. Good aspects to Venus and Jupiter, as long as they are not rulers of the 4th, 6th or 8th houses improves even the most desperate of illnesses, and gives respite.

- When the Moon comes to a trine or sextile of the Ascendant ruler, or ruler of the 11th, 9th or 10th, the condition may be eased.

- If the Moon separates from a weak malevolent planet, and applies to a strong benevolent planet, there is hope for recovery.

- If the Moon is strong when she comes to the square, or opposition of the place of the decumbiture, the sick recovers, if the Moon is aspected to no other planet.

- It is not a good sign if the Moon is eclipsed when she comes to the quartile or opposition to the place she was at the decumbiture.

- If the Moon is afflicted on a critical day by Saturn and Mars or ruler of 8th or 4th, the disease increases. However, there may be ameliorating factors such as at the time of the crisis the Moon beholds the ruler of the Ascendant or Venus or Jupiter.

- If on a critical day the Moon is in dignity, though void of course, there may be fear of a grievous illness, but there is a chance the sick will recover.

- It is very bad when the Moon carries light of the ruler of the Ascendant to the ruler of the 8th, since it threatens death, but not in every case.

- If after the beginning of a disease the Moon opposes an Ascendant ruler that is retrograde or combust, this suggests a disease not easily curable.

- If the Moon comes to square, conjunct or opposition to the planets below, the patient takes a while to recover since the medicines may not be effective.
    (a) The planet afflicting the Ascendant
    (b) The ruler of the Ascendant
    (c) The Moon at the decumbiture
    (d) The ruler of the sixth

- A void of course Moon may suggest that there will be no change in the patient's condition for some length of time. However, if at the next crisis the Moon is sextile or trine Jupiter or Venus, there is chance of recovery.

- If the Moon crosses a sign barrier in transit and is still VOC, then clearly something will happen: the patient's condition will change for better or worse. It will depend how the Moon fares in any particular sign. Naturally it will act well in its own nature if it is in Cancer, its domicile, or in Taurus, its exaltation. It will feel less comfortable in its detriment in Capricorn or in its fall in Scorpio.

- When the Moon comes to a square, conjunction or opposition to a planet afflicting the ruler of the 6th house or a planet therein, the patient deteriorates and medicines might be ineffective.

- When the Moon comes to a trine or sextile of the ruler of the Ascendant, or rulers of the 9th, 10th or 11th, it brings ease.

- If on one of the crisis days the Moon is conjunct, square or opposition to Saturn, Mars or the ruler of the 8th or 4th house, consequences may be dire.

Crisis Days Involving the Sun

If the illness does not terminate by the time the Moon returns to the same place as the decumbiture, it becomes a chronic disease and is then judged by the movement of the Sun.

> *If the disease does not terminate after one month, then it turns chronic, and must be judged by the sun, every time it becomes square or opposition to its place at Decumbiture.*[15]

- The first crisis day would be the 90th day of the disease, or around three months, when the transit Sun is in square to its original decumbiture position.

- If the Sun is in dignity on a critical day, the situation looks hopeful (the reverse if in debility).

- The condition of the Sun on a critical day should be noted with regard to the meeting with the Fortunes or Infortunes.

Revision
1. To which time spans do cardinal, fixed and mutable signs refer?
2. If the Ascendant ruler is slow in motion, is the illness likely to be quick to depart?
3. What do late degrees of a sign on 6th house cusp indicate?
4. What effect does a retrograde Mercury have on health?
5. Which planet tends to lengthen disease and produce chronic infirmities?
6. If the Ascendant ruler is in the 6th house, and the 6th house ruler is in the Ascendant, is the disease likely to be long or short?
7. What aspect does the Moon make at the first critical day after the original decumbiture?
8. How should the sick fare if the Moon translates from a malefic planet to a benefic planet?
9. If the transit Moon crosses from one sign into another, say Taurus, would the change be for better or worse, and why?
10. If the disease is monitored by the Sun, how long after the inception of the disease, or the setting up of the first decumbiture chart, would the first crisis day be?

References
1. AJD, p.97. CA, pp.248, 267.
2. AJD, pp.100-1. CA, p.267.
3. AJD, p.97.
4. CA, p.250.
5. ibid.
6. AJD, p.NC 101.
7. ibid p.C96.
8. EMA, p99.
9. CA, p.258.
10. AJD p.96.
11. CA, p 59.
12. AJD, p.31.
13. CA, p.266.
14. AJD, pp.103-7. CA, pp.255, 267.
15. AJD, p.41.

16

Plants, Aromatics and Astrology

Physick without astrology being like a Lamp without Oyl
'The English Physician', N. Culpeper [1]

Planetary Association

The ancient pharmacopoeia associated plants and aromatics with astrology. Plants were grouped under the different planets, their properties of smell, colour, structure and action upon the body were under the guidance of the celestial orbs. This was the macrocosm reflected in the microcosm.

For instance, plants like ginger, garlic and mustard were associated with the fiery, hot planet Mars due to their pungent aroma and heating effect upon the body.

> *The herbs which we attribute to Mars are such as come near to rednesse, whose leaves are pointed and sharp, whose taste is costick and burning, love to grow in dry places, are corrosive and penetrating the flesh and bones with a subtle heat.*[2]

In contrast calm and collected Venus had dominion over plants such as violet, which apparently have a cooling effect upon the body.

The association of plants and planets seemed to have reached its zenith during the seventeenth century, where the greatest exponent of the art was the herbalist Nicholas Culpeper (1616-1664). He suggested that every disease was ruled by a particular planet, and could be cured by an herb also ruled by that planet.

For instance, the brain could be helped by herbs of Mercury, the breast (lungs) and liver by herbs of Jupiter, thereby enhancing the sanguine humour which in turn would preserve the balance of the other humours. The heart was helped by herbs of the Sun. This is healing by sympathy. Healing may also be carried out by antipathy, that is by opposites. For instance, diseases of Jupiter could be cured by herbs of Mercury and vice versa. Or the disease of the Sun and Moon could be helped by herbs of Saturn, or those of Mars by herbs of Venus and vice versa. Deciding which approach to use was an art in itself and a decumbiture chart was thought to be helpful in this regard.

Planets were also assigned to the organs of plants.[3] These are as follows:

> Saturn *roots*
> Jupiter *fruit*
> Mars *thorns, twigs, bark*
> Sun *stem*
> Venus *flowers*
> Mercury *seed*
> Moon *leaves*

By the end of the 17th century, a scientific approach to plant classification was introduced. Botanists such as the English John Ray (1627-1705) and Swedish Carl Linnaeus (1707-1770) categorized plants by their sexual characteristics. Further, the virtues of a plant were no longer assigned to a mystical deity but were judged upon their chemical constituents.

Nevertheless, a decumbiture chart may suggest to the qualified herbalist, aromatherapist, therapist or healer, at least a possible choice of medication. Besides herbs, Culpeper used aromatic healing oils in his practice, referring to them as 'chemycal oils'.

Planetary Aromatics
Aromatics as a form of healing have a long-forgotten genesis. Aromatic woods and incense were thrown on hot coals and the perfumed smoke ascended heavenwards to greet the gods. The word 'perfume' is derived from the Latin 'per fumin' meaning 'through smoke'. From an evolutionary viewpoint smell is one of the most primitive and yet most important of the senses. Survival for the ancients depended upon their ability to seek out food often by smell and guard against predators.

The aromatic part of the plant is found in the minute glands in either the blossoms, leaves, stems or roots, based on chemical constituents which are the healing source of essential oils. Aromatics have been found to create a mood-altering effect on the human brain. The volatile molecules released into the air pass through the nasal passages to the olfactory centres in the brain. The nerves of the olfactory receptors terminate directly in the limbic system which controls the emotions as well as memory, thirst, hunger and sex.

The use of aromatics in the form of volatile oils extracted from plants began a few centuries before Culpeper's time. Plants might be classed as *nervines* which help calm the nervous system such as chamomile and lavender; and *stimulants* which increase energy and activities of the body, with a pronounced effect upon the digestive, respiratory and circulatory systems, include fennel, rosemary and lemon.

Before modern science, the seven planets were deemed to rule over the aroma of plants designated 'savours', describing the sense of taste. Taste and smell are linked since the smell of food activates the gastric juices.

Astrologer William Lilly gives us the following description of 'savours':[4]

The Sun, which apparently gives "*a mixture of sour and sweet together, or the aromatical flavour, being a little bitter and stiptical (contracting) but withal confortative and a little sharp*" rules such oils as frankincense and myrrh.

The Moon gives us no aromatic delights since it is "*fresh, or without any savour*". Such watery plants as cucumber, cabbage and melon typify the Moon's smell or lack of it. On the other hand Mercury "*doth quicken the spirits*" and is "*subtle and penetrative*". Obviously the scent is piercing, clear and refreshing. Typical of this pervasive aroma is lavender and marjoram.

Venus of course would be "*pleasing and toothsome (delicious) and usually moist and sweet or what is very delectable; in smells what is unctuous (oily) and aromatical, and incites to wantoness*". Venus therefore has a sweet, seductive almost cloying aroma, quite evident in rose, geranium, narcissus and violet. What else can we expect from Mars but to be "*bitter and sharp*", just like the aroma of basil, ginger and pepper. Is there not a hint of spice in them all?

The Greater Benefic, Jupiter, is very much like the Lesser Benefic, Venus, in that it is sweet but perhaps not so cloying. This might be true of linden blossom and jasmine. Lilly makes no bones about Saturn's aroma. It is "*Sour, bitter and sharp*", not too dissimilar from Mars, both Infortunes. Cypress and cumin rather typify the acetic Saturn.

Gathering Herbs

Plants for healing were deemed more efficacious if they were gathered at the right time of day or night, when the sap was rising, and their potency or virtue or subtle essence was high. Jasmine for instance, is gathered at night when the blooms release their fragrance more intensely than in the day time.

Certain plants were deemed to be at their highest potency when gathered in accordance with a particular planetary hour. This referred to the rotation of the Earth in a 24-hour day, where each hour came under one of the seven traditional planets.

The time between sunrise and sunset on any particular day is divided into 12 parts. The first hour after sunrise is ruled by the planet ruling the day, therefore the first hour of Saturday would be ruled by *Saturn*. Thereafter the second hour would be ruled by the planet in increasing speed, which would be *Jupiter*, the third hour by *Mars*, the fourth by the *Sun*, the fifth by *Venus*, the sixth by *Mercury*, the seventh by the *Moon*. The eighth hour would begin again with *Saturn*.

Naturally, the time of sunrise and sunset differs at different times of year, so the actual 'planetary hours' would start at different times and not always be exactly 60 minutes long.

Planetary Hours
Saturn, Jupiter, Mars, Sun, Venus, Mercury, Moon

Planetary Days
Sunday – Sun
Monday – Moon
Tuesday – Mars
Wednesday – Mercury
Thursday – Jupiter
Friday – Venus
Saturday – Saturn

Culpeper gave specific indications for gathering herbs. For instance, a Sun-ruled herb like angelica, would be at its most potent *"when the Sun is in Leo, the Moon applying to his good aspect, in the hour of the Sun or in the hour of Jupiter"*.[5]

Not everyone can wait however until the planets are in exactly the right position before gathering or administering a beneficent remedy!

Temperature of Plants

The temperature of healing plants according to Culpeper[6] in his herbal were either hot, cold, moist, dry or temperate, *"but not of themselves"*, rather in relation to the effect they had on the body of man. 'Cold plants' were so called because the degree of their heat fell below the heat of the body, a 'hot plant' supposedly maintained the heat of the body. Basically, hot plants warmed the body, cold herbs cooled it down, and those that were classified temperate worked no change at all, apparently.

The temperature of herbs was originally classified by Galen: marigold ruled by the Sun, was hot and dry in the first degree, whereas garlic ruled by Mars was hot and dry in the fourth degree, that is, much hotter. So according to the assessment of the relative strength of the humours in the body of the patient, the herbalist would either use hot herbs to counteract a cold condition, or dry herbs to counteract a moist condition.

Herbs hot in the first degree are apparently of equal strength with the human body, restoring its normal temperature, if it had taken a chill. Herbs in the same category might be used to ease perspiration or abate inflammations and fevers. *Herbs hot in the second degree* exceed normal body temperature. These plants are just above normal temperature, have a slightly more pronounced effect on the body and appear to have a detoxifying action. *Herbs hot in the third degree* have a more drastic action, they heat the body and cause strong fevers in order to purge the body of toxins. *Herbs hot in the fourth degree* might even burn the body if outwardly applied, such is their powerful use in heating the body.

Herbs cold in the first degree calm the digestion, abate fevers and refresh the spirits. Possibly those *cold in the second degree* are a little more potent. Those *cold in the third degree* reduce inflammation, refresh perspiration and keep the spirits from fainting. Those that are *cold in the fourth degree* are such as to stupefy the sinuses it seems, and are used in violent pain where life is despaired of.

The classification was a little more complex in that a hot or cold medicine might be moist or dry, though either in the *first, second, third* or *fourth* degree. The *fourth* was the most potent, its action often quite drastic. Ultimately it is just as well to be aware that plants/oils vary in their degree of potency.

Minerals' association with astrology
Initially the attributes given to plants were anecdotal, though chemical analysis of ingredients of plants have often substantiated their past lore. In contrast the healing quality of minerals, or healing crystals, generally remains subjective. Yet as the symbolic meaning of minerals became part of the collective unconscious, their psychological or psychic qualities were thought to have an effect on the body and mind. Names for minerals may seem romanticised like rose quartz, but that surely has more emotional resonance than referring to it as one part silicon to two parts oxygen with a trace of titanium, which is of course its chemical constituent.

There is a direct link between minerals and astrology, since the Sun, Moon and stars, as well as the Earth are all rocks, as well as gasses. The Greek philosopher Anaxagorus stated this as far back as 500BC.[7] As we now know, all are based on the elements and atoms, the building blocks of matter. One reason attributable to the minerals' facility for healing is their ability to transmit and absorb light from the Sun.

There is a very potent link between human beings, the Earth and the Sun. The Earth's equator inclines 23½ degrees towards the Sun in its orbit around the solar disc which reflects the inclination of the human heart towards the left side of the body also at 23½ degrees. So we have a direct link with the Sun, the Earth and the human heart. In astrology, the Sun is associated with the heart.

Each kingdom in nature draws its life force from the succeeding one. The mineral kingdom feeds the vegetable kingdom through the mineral content in the earth; the vegetable kingdom feeds the animal and human kingdom and the former two are at the disposal of the human kingdom.

> The mineral kingdom
> The vegetable kingdom
> The animal kingdom
> The human kingdom
> Kingdom of souls

The mineral kingdom came into existence through the agency of fire, stolen from the gods by Prometheus to give to man, as the myth goes. Fire fuels the volcanic actions which change the surface of the earth, and crystals reveal themselves. The mineral kingdom apparently represents the divine plan behind our existence, which is hidden in the geometry of a crystal, its beauty due to its radiant colour.[8]

The seven colours, as Isaac Newton demonstrated, are contained within a ray of light (as seen through a prism). The variance of colour in crystals depends upon absorption and transmission of light through individual crystals. Neither does light travel with the same velocity through the various crystals, thus allowing an interesting play of light. In astrology the Sun and Moon are termed the Lights, since one shines by day and the other by night. The Lights, or the Sun and Moon, are also associated with the eyes which receive light.

Planetary rulership of plants and minerals is a guide or an aid to selection for self or a client, and ultimately choice must always rest with the practitioner/astrologer.

Revision
1. Which planet's herbs might help the brain?
2. What does healing by antipathy mean? Give an example.
3. Which planet rules the plant organ's twigs and barks?
4. To which planet were herbs good for the heart assigned?
5. Which planet's aroma is described as 'sour, bitter and sharp'?
6. Which planet might rule cooling herbs?
7. Why was it thought that it was important to gather herbs at a specific time?
8. Which planet rules the first hour after sunrise on Wednesday?
9. How was the temperature of plants categorized?
10. Which was the hottest or coldest degree, the first or fourth?

References
1. CH, p.210.
2. CA, p.67.
3. BI, p.236.

4. CA, pp.57-83.
5. CH, p.8.
6. ibid pp.376-380.
7. Cooper, P. *The Healing Power of Light*, Piatkus, 2000.
8. Bailey A. *Esoteric Psychology 1*, Lucis Press, 1936/1970 pp.226-227.

17

Materia Medica

Traditional Planetary Rulerships of Plants, Essential Oils and Minerals

There's Rosemary, that's for remembrance
'Hamlet', Act 4, Scene 5, William Shakespeare

The rulership of plants, as well as minerals, has been taken from the works of Claude Dariot, William Lilly, Nicholas Culpeper, and Joseph Blagrave, 16th/17th century astrologers who had translated earlier works from the Latin and Arabic. Some information is based on Al-Biruni's work from the 12th century. The authors are not always in agreement!

It is as well to remember that the association of plant with planet was often based purely on appearance. The lilac/blue flowers of thyme might be herbs of Venus with its pacifying nature. Mars herbs or plants were hot and prickly, and Mercury herbs often had wispy fronds, such as dill. Although some plants do indeed bear the qualities assigned to its ruling planet, it is just as well to keep an open mind in judgment.

Plants marked with a star* do not have a traditional ruler; their placement under a particular planet is purely conjecture. Reasons for the assignment are given usually due to the prime effect on one of the bodily systems.

THE SUN
Aroma "*A mixture of sour and sweet together, or the aromatical flavour, being a little bitter and stiptical (contracting) but withal confortative and a little sharp.*"[1]
Humour Hot and dry.
Physiology Blood, heart, brain, cerebro-spinal nervous system, circulation system, spleen, the eyes, and the back particularly the thoracic area, oxygenation, right side of the body, chronic diseases, the cells of the body. Since the Sun represents the vital spirits in the chart, it is always good to use a remedy that strengthens the Sun, according to Culpeper.

Positive Main effect is cordial, that is, a tonic for the heart. It is also stimulant, preservative and sudorific.
Negative Inflammatory, drying, fevers, haemorrhage.

Angelica
Planet The Sun
Botany Distilled from the seeds and roots of the herb angelica archangelica.
Uses It has a slightly musky aroma, a hot plant and considered a base note. It would appear to have a grounding quality and is a very drying oil.[2] It appears to have a stimulating and vitalising effect upon the body, and is therefore good in states of bodily depletion. It is commonly used for insomnia, nervous exhaustion, rheumatism and psoriasis. Apparently it stimulates oestrogen.[3] In herbal remedies it is used as a tonic for the heart.
Caution Avoid using in pregnancy and diabetes, and before exposure to the sun.

Bergamot*
Planet The Sun?
Botany Distilled from the peel/fruit of the citrus bergamia tree.
Uses Bergamot seems to have links with the urinary tract, chiefly cystitis. It also works on the digestive tract and relieves conditions such as painful digestion, dyspepsia, flatulence, indigestion. It is a general tonic for the intestines, as well as for the lungs and respiration and is an excellent insect repellent. It seems to have a reputation for soothing skin eruptions. It is helpful for depression and its uplifting quality may link it to the Sun.
Caution It may irritate sensitive skin. Strong sunlight should be avoided after use as it increases photosensitivity.

Cedarwood
Planet The Sun
Botany Distilled from the wood and sawdust of the cedrus atlantica tree.
Uses It has a slightly woody aroma and acts as a base note. Where it seems to reflect some of the Sun's qualities, is in its 'drying' and possibly 'heating' action. For instance, it has a curbing action on excess phlegm and cold conditions, acting by antipathy. In the same way it helps to regulate oily conditions of the skin and hair, such as acne and seborrhoea. Dryness and long-standing ailments are assigned to Saturn, and some people feel that cedarwood has a link to this planet. It is also said to be helpful with cystitis.
Caution Not to be used in pregnancy.

Chamomile
Planet The Sun
Botany Distilled from the flowers of the herbs Roman (anthemis nobilis) and German (matricaria chamomilla).
Uses The Roman variety has an apple-like aroma, and thought to be a middle note. It is said to be hot like the Sun yet it has a reputation for cooling inflammatory skin conditions such as acne, eczema and allergies generally. This appears to be acting by sympathy and is even more true of German chamomile with its azulene constituent, known for its cooling action on inflammation. In the same way it is said to be helpful for rheumatism.[4] Though it has a tonic effect on the body, it appears to be a more soothing plant and oil rather than a stimulating one. It has a reputation for helping with the digestive and reproductive systems and is often used for children's ailments particularly in promoting sleep.
Caution Be careful with sensitive skin, and in pregnancy.

Frankincense
Planet The Sun
Botany Distilled from the bark of the boswellia carteria/thurifera shrub.
Uses It has a woody, slightly spicy aroma with a faint citrus note, and a base note. Certainly in ancient times it was a king amongst incense, hence its name 'real incense' (real in Latin means royal) and the Sun represents royalty. It may be a very good oil to use in meditation, energy work and healing on the subtle level, meaning balancing the subtle bodies: etheric, emotional and mental. When these subtle levels of the body are in balance, the physical body follows suit. Frankincense is also said to stimulate cell regeneration and is therefore good in skin preparations, and of course the Sun rules cells. It is also associated with pulmonary problems, and the urinary system.
Caution Not known

Galbanum
Planet The Sun
Botany Distilled from the resin of the ferula galbaniflua shrub.
Uses Musk-like, pungent, evocative of damp woodlands, its aroma is very immediate, a top note, but it tends to linger, so some say it is a base note. It has a reputation for dealing with chronic ailments especially freeing mucous and calming bronchial spasm. It seems to have an effect on gynaecological problems such as menopausal difficulties, hot flushes, irritable moods, menstrual cramp, as well as lack of periods. It may be beneficial for intractable skin problems, and mature skins.
Caution Best avoided in pregnancy. Its strong, lingering aroma may induce headaches, and irritate mucous membranes. May irritate sensitive skin.

Grapefruit*
Planet The Sun?
Botany From the peel of citrus paradisi.
Uses Grapefruit has an uplifting citrus aroma, and is a top note. It has a reputation as a lymphatic stimulant, nourishing the tissues and controlling liquid processes, which seems to incline it to rulership of the Sun. It works well on the digestive system, acting as a tonic and a cleanser, and is well known as an appetite stimulant. It appears to have a soothing effect on the body and may help with headaches, migraine, and easing pre-menstrual tension.
Caution Skin irritation may occur if exposed to strong sunlight.

Juniper
Planet The Sun
Botany Distilled from the berries of the juniperus communis bush.
Uses Juniper has a slightly woody, refreshing aroma, a middle note, and is said to be a hot oil. Its main quality seems to be detoxification, ridding the body and skin of congestion and toxins. And so much so that it was once thought to be effective against the plague. It has a beneficial effect on the genito-urinary system, and sluggish digestion. Culpeper mentions that there is *"scarce a better remedy for wind in any part of the body, or the colic, than the chymical oil (essential oil) drawn from the berries."*[5] It seems to help gout and sciatica and is a tonic to the mind and body.
Caution Prolonged use may over-stimulate the kidneys and should be avoided in cases of severe kidney disease or other inflammatory conditions. It is best avoided during pregnancy and may be a slight irritant on some skins.

Lemon
Planet The Sun
Botany Distilled from the peel of the citrus limonum fruit.
Uses Lemon has a fresh citrus aroma and a sharp top note. It is a superb tonic for the circulatory system, apparently stimulating the white corpuscles and so invigorating the immune system to aid the body fight infectious disease. It also appears to stem external bleeding. It would seem therefore that there is a strong link to the Sun and the heart. Indeed, Culpeper saw it as a cordial. It may also have an effect on cold conditions. It is said also to relieve headaches, refresh the vital spirits, and help keep infection at bay.
Caution May irritate sensitive skin.

Lemongrass*
Planet The Sun?
Botany Oil distilled from the grasses of cymbopogon citratus.
Uses It gives a boost to the nervous system and acts as a revitalising tonic to the body, which may be helpful after illness. Invigorating the body may suggest a link to the Sun. It is purportedly helpful for digestive problems and encourages appetite and is said to help stem the tide on contagious diseases, and is helpful with sore throats.
Caution It is a very strong oil and may irritate sensitive skins. Small doses are preferable.

Lime*
Planet The Sun?
Botany Distilled from the fruit of the citrus aurantifolia tree.
Uses Lime has a strong sharp citrus aroma, and top note. It appears to have a beneficial effect on colds; it warms the body and lifts the spirits. It seems to be helpful for greasy skin, sores and warts and also has a reputation for helping poor circulation. It is useful therefore with varicose veins, as well as rheumatic conditions.
Caution May be photo-toxic in full sun.

Myrrh
Planet The Sun
Botany Distilled from the resin of the commiphora myrrha bush.
Uses Myrrh has a smoky, gum-like, slightly musky aroma, and appears to have a 'drying' action like the Sun. It is decidedly a base oil. It is principally effective against mucous in the lungs and likely to be helpful for the respiratory system: ailments include catarrh, pharyngitis and coughs. It is reputedly helpful for throat and mouth problems such as gingivitis, spongy gums, and bad breath and seems to have an effect on gynaecological problems. It reputedly stimulates white blood corpuscles and invigorates the immune system, which again seems to be associated with the Sun.
Caution It is an emmenagogue so best avoided in pregnancy.

Neroli*
Planet The Sun?
Botany Distilled from the flowers of the orange tree, citrus vulgaris, aurantium.
Uses Neroli has a subtle floral fragrance but is not too sweet; a middle note, sometimes used as a top note. It seems to have a connection with the heart in so much as it soothes palpitations and calms down the mind and body in cases of stress. It has a rather hypnotic effect, which is helpful for nervous

tension, insomnia, even period cramp due to its antispasmodic action.
Caution Not too good for focused work.

Orange
Planet The Sun
Botany Distilled from the peel of the orange tree, citrus aurantium.
Uses A sharp, sweet, refreshing fragrance; a top note. It may quell heart palpitations, and seems to have a beneficial effect on the circulation. It appears to have a pronounced effect upon the digestive system, dealing with constipation and diarrhoea alike. It is said to strengthen the gums and have an effect on mouth ulcers. It has a reputation for bringing down temperature. A gentle tonic on the mind, it also has the ability to deal with depression. Certainly it is an uplifting, 'sunny' type of oil.
Caution Prolonged use may irritate sensitive skin, and there is a chance of photo toxicity as well.

Petitgrain*
Planet The Sun?
Botany Distilled from the leaves of the orange tree, citrus aurantium.
Uses A slightly woody yet floral fragrance, a top to middle note. It seems to sedate the nervous system and is helpful for rapid heart beat. It may slow the body down. However at the same time it has a reputation for being helpful in debilitated states. Apparently it has a balancing effect on the skin.
Caution Not known.

Rosemary
Planet The Sun
Botany Distilled from the flowers of the herb, rosmarinus officialis.
Uses A refreshing herbal fragrance, and quite piercing. Top to middle note. It is valued as a heart tonic and cardiac stimulant as well as normalising low blood pressure. It is apparently excellent for anaemia, and helps breathing and the circulation. Culpeper says it *"helps all cold diseases"*.[6] as well as the *"chymical oil being good for all diseases of the head"*. But warns that it is *"very quick and piercing and only a little be taken at a time"*. Certainly it has a reputation for energising and activating the brain in cases of exhaustion. It also has a reputation for being a liver tonic and it boosts the digestion. It is said to relieve menstrual cramp and normalise periods and its pain-relieving properties may be helpful with rheumatic pain.
Caution Very stimulating, so perhaps not suitable for people with high blood pressure. Best avoided in pregnancy. May antidote homeopathic remedies.

Rosewood*
Planet The Sun?
Botany From the leaves of the rosdeaodora var.amazonica, evergreen tree.
Uses It seems to have a tonic on the body and is helpful in cases of exhaustion, particularly after illness. Its immuno-stimulant properties incline it to the Sun. It has head clearing qualities and seems to act on head colds. It is often used in skin complaints and seems to have a clearing effect on the skin. It is helpful in cases of depression.
Caution Not known.

Spikenard
Planet The Sun
Botany From the root of the herb nardostachys jatamansi.
Uses A deep, earthy, herby, very pungent aroma, and a base note. Dioscorides termed it as *"warming and drying"*, which is linked to the Sun. Apparently it is hot and dry and diuretic, digestive and has an effect on headcolds. Also deemed to have a regenerative effect on the skin. Historically it was used in religious rituals as an anointing oil, possibly in harmonizing the three subtle bodies. It is thought to be a balancing oil generally and appears to help with inflammation, gynaecological problems, and in detoxification. Spikenard had a reputation for healing epilepsy, hysteria and other convulsions.
Caution Spikenard is not an essential oil of great popularity perhaps because it has a very overpowering, pungent aroma and should be used sparingly.

THE MOON
Aroma *"Fresh, or without any savour"*.[7]
Humour Cold and Moist. Apparently the Moon is at its most cold and moist in her last quarter.
Physiology Breasts, stomach and womb, liquids of the body. Linked to the lymphatic system, lacteals, digestion, fluids, right brain functions (imagination), parturition, the eye particularly the left eye in man, right in woman, absorbent vessels.
Positive Stomachic mainly, nutritive, fertile, cleansing, cooling, regulating female functions, emetic.
Negative Putrefaction, dissolving, variable, haemorrhage, mental instability, oedema, lack of tone, mutational, disintegrating.

Clary Sage
Planet The Moon
Botany Distilled from the flowering tops of the herb salvia sclarea.
Uses A slightly pungent, earthy aroma, distinctly herby. A top to middle note, thought to be a hot oil. It has a beneficial effect on the digestion, reputedly aiding wind and gastric spasm and is said to be beneficial for gynaecological problems, easing menstrual tension as well as cramp and scanty periods. It is thought to be a hormone balancer, and may well help with post natal depression and fertility problems. Since the Moon rules fluids, it is interesting that it also helps with excessive perspiration.
Caution Its sedative quality can dull the senses and should not be used before driving or working machinery. Continual usage may produce headaches. Nausea may occur if alcohol is consumed.

MERCURY
Aroma *"Doth quicken the spirits, and is subtle and penetrative."*[8]
Humour Ordinarily considered a cold and dry planet, tending towards the melancholic humour. It is dry when in a masculine sign; moist in a feminine sign. Mercury is masculine when oriental of the Sun, and feminine when occidental (rising after the Sun, more degrees; rising before the Sun, less degrees). It rules Gemini and Virgo, the lungs, the arms, hands and intestines. It has a dual nature and is influenced by aspects of the other planets.
Physiology The nervous system, an affinity with the senses.
Positive Pectoral, cephalic, nervine, alterative, cholagogue, chylification.
Negative Mental illness, epilepsy, nerves, impulsive, sleeplessness, restlessness. Irregular course of diseases, cellular irritation. Impediments in speech. Neuralgia. There could be nerve problems in the area of the body as indicated by the sign Mercury is in.

Cardomom*
Planet Mercury?
Botany Distilled from the dried ripe fruit of the elettaria cardomomum spice herb.
Uses The main action appears to be on the digestive system, particularly heartburn, flatulence and indigestion. It has some effect on the nervous system such as mental fatigue and nervous tension. It appears to be a stimulating oil, and warming, so there is some connection with the Sun and Mercury.
Caution Be careful with dosage as it may cause skin allergy.

Fennel, Sweet
Planet Mercury
Botany Distilled from the seeds of the foeniculum vulgare herb.
Uses It has a liquorice-like herby aroma, and thought to be a top to middle note, and a hot oil. Culpeper mentions that it *"consumes the phlegmatic humour"*,[9] so it is helpful for congestion and colds. Culpeper also says that fennel has affinity with Virgo particularly, the sign which rules the small intestines. It quells nausea and helps to relieve flatulence, and is a tonic for the liver, spleen and gall. It also appears to have excellent detoxifying properties, especially from over-eating and alcohol and is thought to be a blood cleanser. It may also be helpful with gynaecological problems since it is said to imitate the hormone oestrogen. Purportedly has an effect on the genital-urinary system.
Caution A powerful oil, easily subject to toxicity with overuse. It may cause skin sensitisation in some individuals. Those pregnant or suffering from epilepsy should avoid it. Avoid Bitter Fennel, as it is too toxic.

Lavender
Planet Mercury
Botany Distilled from the flowers of the lavendula officinalis herb.
Uses A fresh, floral aroma, thought to be a hot oil and a middle note. Its effect on the nervous system is well known, having a balancing effect, and according to Rudolf Steiner it balances the subtle bodies too. Lavender is commonly used where a relaxing, sedative but uplifting oil is needed. It may not always be the first choice for the respiratory system, but it apparently has an effect on bronchitis, asthma, catarrh and colds. This of course links with Mercury's 'pectorals'.
Caution Avoid in pregnancy to be on the safe side, especially the first three months.

Marjoram
Planet Mercury
Botany Distilled from the heads and leaves of the origanum marjorana herb.
Uses A warm, slightly spicy penetrating aroma, thought to be a hot oil and a middle note. It accords with Mercury since it has a strong reputation for dealing with bronchial conditions and helps to clear head colds. It has a calming effect on the nervous system and a warming effect on the emotions. It warms up muscles especially where there is stiffness, dilates arteries allowing easier flow of blood, and it is a good tonic to the blood and lowers high blood pressure. It has a soothing effect on the digestion and could help with constipation, flatulence, nausea, and could be helpful with sea-

sickness. Generally it is a very versatile oil, just like the planet which rules it.
Caution Prolonged use can cause drowsiness and it is best avoided in pregnancy.

Origano
Planet Mercury
Botany From the leaves of the herb origanum vulgare.
Uses Like so many herbs, the main effect seems to be on the digestive system, particularly in combating acidity, as well as calming intestinal spasm. Also appears to act on the respiratory system and is helpful for colds, catarrh and bronchitis. Its stimulating action may be beneficial to head colds, as well as migraine, deafness, pain, tinnitus, and toothache. It is a versatile oil, said to be helpful for muscular pain, waterlogged tissues and rheumatism.
Caution As an essential oil it is very potent and could irritate the mucous membranes. Best avoided in pregnancy and some say best avoided altogether.

Valerian
Planet: Mercury
Botany Distilled from the root of the valeriana officinalis herb.
Uses A very earthy aroma, apparently a hot oil and a base note. It is also a drying oil apparently. The link to Mercury is very pronounced since its tranquilising action is well known on the nervous system and it has a reputation for being good for insomnia, stress, nervous anxiety and tension. It also has a relaxing effect on the muscles and is said to help urinary problems. It is an expectorant and therefore appears to have a beneficial effect on the lungs to 'loosen things up', in other words it's good for congestion in the body. It releases phlegm and eases coughs.
Caution It has an overpowering aroma and should be used sparingly in a synergistic mix. May cause lethargy in prolonged use.

VENUS
Aroma *"Pleasing and toothsome (delicious) and usually moist and sweet or what is very delectable; in smells what is unctuous (oily) and aromatical, and incites to wantoness."*[10]
Humour Cold and moist.
Physiology The kidneys and glandular system, reproductive system, venous circulation, semen, fevers.
Positive Feminine, fruitful, homeostasis, nutrition, cell building, conserving, demulcent, emetic, erotic, feminine, nutritious, rhythmical, diuretic, aphrodisiac, period of remission in fevers. Medicines which are conglutinating, mollifying and effective to assuage ulcers.

Negative Intemperance, gormandizing, indulgent, lethargic, lustful, plethoric, atrophy, intemperance, skin eruptions, diseases arising from overabundance of moisture.

Coriander
Planet Venus (or Mercury)
Botany Distilled from the fruit and seeds of the coriander sativum herb.
Uses It has a sweet, spicy slightly pungent aroma and is thought to be a hot oil and a top note. It seems to act principally on the digestive system and gives a warming effect on the stomach, stimulating appetite and possibly helpful with eating disorders. It could also be helpful with cold conditions, such as influenza and therefore has a beneficial effect on the lungs. It reputedly clears the body of toxins, fluids wastes and is a general tonic to the body. Apparently it has a tonic effect on the spleen and the glandular and reproductive systems.
Caution It may have a stupefying effect in large doses.

Geranium
Planet Venus
Botany Distilled from the flowers and leaves of the pelargonium odorantissimum/graveolens.
Uses A sweet and heavy aroma, with a middle note. It seems to have a cooling action. It seems to reflect the qualities of Venus in so much as it is often used for feminine conditions such as infertility, premenstrual syndrome and menopausal problems. It is thought to balance the hormonal system. Again its balancing nature accords well with the planet, which is said to bestow harmony. Other qualities include nervous tension and skin conditions.
Caution It is generally safe, though may cause irritation on sensitive skins. It is said to regulate the hormonal system, so is best avoided in pregnancy. Contraindicated apparently for cancer, particularly ovarian and breast cancer.[11]

Myrtle
Planet Venus or Mercury
Botany Distilled from the leaves of the myrtus communis bush.
Uses A fresh, slightly sweet and penetrating aroma, and a middle note. It appears to be a pectoral, linked to Mercury. It has a reputation for having a pronounced clearing effect on pulmonary disorders. However Venus is linked to the phlegmatic humour, the seat of which is in the lungs. It is useful for combating excessive moisture and has a soothing quality, useful for sleep. Its link to the urinary system shows it to be helpful with cystitis. It

also is thought to be useful in clearing congestion of the pelvic organs, and is reputedly a tonic to the womb, as well as the intestines.
Caution It could possibly irritate mucous membranes with prolonged use.

Palmarose*
Planet Venus?
Botany Distilled from the blooms of the cymbopogon martini bush.
Uses A sweet, slightly dry aroma, with a top to middle note. It is often used in skin care since it is said to have a calming, soothing and regenerating quality. It has a reputation for being a tonic to the digestive system, particularly the intestines. Its calming and uplifting effect is useful in cases of nervous exhaustion and heart palpitations. Its sweet aroma inclines it to Venus but its effect to Mercury.
Caution The very sweet, heady aroma, may give rise to headaches in high dosage.

Peppermint
Planet Venus
Botany Distilled from the mentha piperita herb.
Uses A sharp and piercing aroma, with a top note and thought to be a hot oil. But like Venus it has a balancing action on the body: cooling when hot, warming when cold, especially in head colds and influenza. It reputedly has an effect on kidney as well as liver disorders and is said to relieve constipation, diarrhoea, flatulence, and travel sickness as well as IBS (irritable bowel syndrome), indigestion, nausea and bloating. It apparently relieves muscle tension in the colon calming spasm and is also said to be helpful for joint pain.
Caution Use only on local areas in massage. Keep away from the face as it will sting the eyes. This is definitely a case when less is more. Contraindicated against epileptic sufferers, pregnancy or heart disease.

Rose
Planet Venus
Botany Distilled from the petals of rosa centifolia and rosa damascene.
Uses A deep, sweet and flowery aroma, a middle note and thought to be a cold oil. It seems to have a cooling action on inflammatory conditions. Culpeper saw it as helpful for the heart, and indeed it is supposed to activate sluggish blood circulation, relieve cardiac congestion and tone the capillaries. Myth-wise it is of course a plant long associated with the heart in love's domain, and so linked with Venus. It is an excellent tonic for the womb, calming menstrual tension and regulating the menstrual cycle and is said to help 'male' problems too, such as infertility and impotence. It is a tonic to

the digestive system and apparently helps sooth sore throats, ease coughs and decongest the liver.
Caution Best avoided in pregnancy.

Thyme
Planet Venus (some say Mercury)
Botany Distilled from the flowers and leaves of the thymus vulgaris herb.
Uses A slightly sweet but strong herbal fragrance. A top to middle note, and said to be a hot oil. It seems to have a warming action and is excellent for chest complaints such as coughs, laryngitis and asthma. It is a good immuno-stimulant as well as eliminating phlegm and aiding sore throats. It seems to be a tonic to the circulation and helpful for rheumatic complaints and sciatica. It is also a digestive stimulant and urinary antiseptic. It is purportedly helpful for menstrual difficulties such as scanty periods and leucorrhoea and is apparently helpful in childbirth, speeding delivery and expelling afterbirth, with a cleansing action which could help in cases of miscarriage as well.
Caution It is a strong antiseptic, so be careful of toxicity with overuse, and skin irritation. Avoid in pregnancy or with high blood pressure.

Violet
Planet Venus
Botany An absolute, extracted by enfleurage from the leaves of the viola odorata plant.
Uses Violet leaf has an earthy and dry aroma, not sweet like the flowers. It is a cooling oil and has a middle to base note. No surprise then to find that it apparently cools inflammatory conditions of the body, *"purges the body of choleric humours"*,[12] and deals with any inflammatory swellings in the body. It may be helpful with fevers and skin problems and possibly a tonic and decongestant to the kidneys, liver and bladder, and said to aid cystitis. It helps with lower back pain. It seems to have an effect on the lungs, helping with colds and phlegm and is said to have aphrodisiac properties too. Quite a Venusian oil!
Caution Not known.

Yarrow
Planet Venus
Botany Distilled from the achillea millefolium herb.
Uses Slightly sweet with a hint of spice, a top note, and thought to be a cooling oil. It links with Venus due to its reputation as a tonic to the reproductive system. It appears to have a hormonal action and deals with irregular menstruation, heavy periods, menopausal problems, inflammation of

the ovaries, prolapsed of the womb, and fibroids. It is beneficial for digestive problems such as flatulence, indigestion, IBS, bloating, and it improves sluggish digestion. It is also helpful with feverish colds and congestion of the head, and it promotes perspiration. A tonic to the urinary system, it helps the flow of urine, and has some pain relieving properties.
Caution It may have a photosensitising action in the sun.

Ylang Ylang*
Planet Venus
Botany Distilled from the flowers of a tropical tree, cananga odorata.
Uses A reputed hormone balancer and said to be helpful with the reproductive system. It has a reputation for keeping the breasts firm. All in all it appears to help with sexual problems such as impotence and frigidity, and with its reputation as an aphrodisiac inclines it to Venus. Its antiseptic action may well have a beneficial effect on intestinal infections and it may help to bring down high blood pressure due to its sedative qualities. A good oil to encourage hair growth, and a tonic to the scalp.
Caution Excessive use may lead to headaches and nausea. Could irritate sensitive skins.

MARS
Aroma *"Bittersweet and sharp."*[13]
Humour Hot and dry.
Physiology Muscular system, haemoglobin, generative organs, rectum, poisons, smell, a sharp quality.
Positive Rubefacient, driving energy and heating from the centre out, drawing blood to the surface. Cleansing body by promoting fevers and burning up the impurities of the system, dissolving obstructions. Accelerates bodily systems, therefore a stimulant, tonic, astringent giving way to dryness.
Negative Acute diseases, inflammatory conditions, fevers, skin eruptions, acute, dry, pungent odours. Causes hot diseases such as measles, scarlet fever, erysipelas, typhus. Caustic, acidic, piercing ailments, barren, high blood pressure.

Basil, Sweet
Planet Mars
Botany Distilled from the tops and leaves of the ocimum basilicum herb.
Uses Clear, slightly liquorice-like aroma, a top note. Basil seems to have a stimulating and tonic effect on most systems of the body and a reputation for relieving deep muscle spasm, so it accords with the Mars rulership. Its cephalic properties are helpful with migraine and headaches, fainting spells and temporary paralysis. It is effective on the respiratory system, restoring

sense of smell due to catarrh, and helpful with digestive disorders as well as beneficial to the intestines and kidneys. It seems to help with gynaecological problems and appears to soothe bee stings and insect bites.

Caution It is stimulating, but may have a stupefying effect when used in excess. Less is more with this essential oil. Best to avoid in pregnancy, and may irritate sensitive skin.

Black Pepper
Planet Mars
Botany Distilled from the fruit of the piper nigrum shrub.
Uses A spicy, sharp aroma, said to be hot and dry, with a middle to top note. The dilation of local blood vessels makes it useful for muscular aches and pains and tired and aching limbs, so it accords well with Mars. It is good for rheumatoid arthritis and temporary paralysis of the limbs. It is reputedly a good oil to use before excessive exertion like sport and also has a reputation for restoring tone to colon muscles. Generally it is a stimulating oil that acts as a tonic on the digestive system, circulatory system and respiratory system.
Caution Too much use may over stimulate the kidneys. Also a possibility of skin irritation.

Ginger
Planet Mars
Botany Distilled from the root of the zingiber officinalis herb.
Uses A sharp and pungent aroma with a hint of lemon, variously reported to be top or base note, and a very hot and drying oil according to Culpeper. It is thought to be helpful in inflammatory conditions such as arthritis, which is healing more by sympathy. It is also a tonic to the circulation. It warms cold conditions such as catarrh and influenza, as well as coughs and sore throats. It is well known for its effect on the digestion, nausea, flatulence and good for travel sickness, as well as morning sickness. It is apparently helpful where there is an excess of moisture: healing by antipathy. It is helpful for nervous exhaustion and general weakness and sharpens the senses.
Caution Its aroma may be a little overpowering, easy on dosage. It may cause skin sensitization on some people.

Pine
Planet Mars
Botany Distilled from the needles and cones of the pinus sylvestris tree.
Uses A fresh, forest fragrance, and a middle note. It does have some reputation for benefiting muscular pain and circulation which accords with

Mars. Gout, sciatica and arthritis are said to benefit. Indeed, it seems to have a revitalising effect upon the body, a tonic to the adrenal glands - ruled by Mars. It appears to have a balancing action in so much as it is warming and cooling depending upon need. However its main claim to fame seems to be its efficacy on respiratory problems. It helps to clear sinuses, eases breathing and has a reputation for a beneficial action on bronchitis, laryngitis and influenza. Its other qualities appear to include a cleansing action on the urinary system, uterus and digestive system. It is helpful for mental fatigue.

Caution Use small doses as it is thought to irritate sensitive skins, so avoid those with skin allergies. Avoid Dwarf Pine (pinus pumilio), a hazardous oil.

Vitex (agnus castus)
Planet Mars
Botany Distilled from the seed of the agnus castus plant
Uses Woody aroma like forest leaves, slightly fungal. Vitex is also called 'Monk's Pepper' because of its hot and dry nature which accords with Blagrave who puts it under a Mars rulership. Gerard, the notable 16th century Renaissance herbalist, referred to Vitex as a female remedy[14] which inclines it to a Moon or Venus rulership, as some modern writers claim, and indeed it is said to be a hormone balancer and has long been used for premenstrual syndrome and period pain. It has also been used historically for epilepsy and mental disorders as well as the digestion, all linked with the Moon. It is helpful for pains in the limbs.

Caution Contraindicated if using oral contraceptives, and HRT, although that may apply more to the herb. Some people have reported headache, nausea and rash, possibly in long usage. Advised against use if using depressants. Not to be used in conjunction with other essential oils and herbs that have hormonal effects.[15]

JUPITER
Aroma *"Sweet and well scented, in no way offensive"*[16]
Humour Hot and moist.
Physiology Mainly hepatic, helpful for liver problems. Arterial blood circulation. Plethoric, metabolic system. Glycogen, fuel for muscular activity. Has a link with lungs.
Positive Medicines that conglutinate, mollify, assuage and cure ulcers, restoration of health, ensure fruitfulness, gives moistness, balsamic, antispasmodic.
Negative Clogging, gluttonous, gormandizing, corrupt blood.

Jasmine
Planet Jupiter
Botany Solvent extraction from the jasminum grandiflorum flowers.
Uses Sweet, flowery and a slightly heady aroma. A middle to base note. It has a reputation for uplifting the emotions, particularly helpful with depression, and this appears to be the only link to Jupiter. Jupiter is a planet of positive thinking and happiness, so Jasmine's reputation for lifting the mood may not be unfounded. Otherwise the oil is linked to its aphrodisiac properties and warming cold conditions , from a more psychological viewpoint perhaps.
Caution Not to be used in pregnancy until about to give birth, since it reputedly helps to ease labour. Its overuse could disturb bodily fluids and its rather heady aroma may slow down concentration.

Linden Blossom
Planet: Jupiter
Botany Extraction by enfleurage from the flowers of the tilia europaea tree.
Uses A slightly sweet, slightly spicy aroma and a base note. Linden blossom links to Jupiter in that it has a reputation for purifying and thinning the blood, which could help with circulatory problems. Apparently it also has a beneficial action on high cholesterol levels, perhaps the herb rather than the oil, and anaemia. Another connection to Jupiter is its apparent detoxifying effect on the liver as well as diuretic effect on the kidneys. It deals with excess urea, and benefits stomach problems and rheumatism.
Caution Slight chance of causing allergy to sensitive skins. The aroma may be a little 'heady' for some.

Melissa
Planet Jupiter
Botany Distilled from the leaves of the melissa officinalis herb.
Uses Sweet and lemon-like aroma with floral undertones. A middle note and thought to be a hot oil. It links to Jupiter by acting on the emotions, by lifting depression. It appears also to have a detoxifying quality, helping to cleanse the blood, a tonic for the liver, which is Jupiter ruled, as well as the spleen. It also seems to help break boils free of pus. Otherwise it has a reputation for calming the heart rate, dealing with fatigue, and is a boon to the female reproductive system, dealing with morning sickness as well as helping to expel afterbirth, and settles the stomach. It seems to balance the body by helping with colds and has a cooling effect on fevers. It eases allergies and has a calming effect on breathing.

Caution As it helps to regulate menstruation, it is best avoided in pregnancy. Also there is the possibility of irritating sensitive skins. Low concentrations are best.

SATURN
Aroma *"Sour, bitter and sharp"*[17]
Humour Cold and dry.
Physiology Skeletal system, chronic ailments, knees, plasma of the foetus.
Positive Medicines that cool or refrigerate. Astringent or binding and clotting, as well as coagulate.
Negative Barren, chronic, crystallizing, depleting, retarding, suppressing. Bruises, falls, contracts, forming uric acid.

Cypress
Planet Saturn
Botany Distilled from the leaves, twigs and cones of the cupressus sempervirens tree.
Uses A woody, clear and refreshing aroma, with a middle to base note. Culpeper says it is a hot oil. It does have Saturn connotations such as its aromatic durability and 'drying' effect, the latter no doubt due to its astringent qualities, since it is useful where there is excess fluid such as haemorrhages, copius bleeding, heavy menstruation, perspiration and oedema. It appears to have a tonic effect on the circulation. In this regard it is helpful with menopausal hot flushes. It also has a reputation for easing rheumatism and muscular spasm.
Caution It regulates the menstrual cycle so is best avoided in pregnancy. Its effect on varicose veins is well known, but care should be taken in applying the oil over this area – a light touch is very necessary, or preferably a compress.

Eucalyptus*
Planet Saturn?
Botany Distilled from the leaves of the eucalyptus tree.
Uses A clear refreshing aroma, most likely a top note, and seems to have a balancing action, cooling when hot, heating when cold. It is well known for helping to clear the respiratory tract principally of mucous and allows easier breathing. It is particularly good for cold conditions, influenza, throat infections, coughs, catarrhal conditions, sinusitis and asthma and it seems to have a reputation for aiding infectious diseases. It may also reduce the effects of migraine. Some relief may be gained for muscular aches and pains and it may help clear the skin. There is some benefit to the genital-urinary system.

Caution Best avoided in high blood pressure, epilepsy. It may antidote homeopathic medicine.

Sandalwood*
Planet Saturn?
Botany Distilled from the heartwood of the santalum album tree.
Uses Could be linked to Saturn due to its reputation, spiritually at least, of cutting the ties that bind with terrestrial life. Indeed it has been burnt at funerals to free the soul. More mundanely it has a strong resistant quality, which is also linked to Saturn. Yet its aroma, slightly drying, is similar to that of cedarwood, which is linked to the Sun. Sandalwood likewise is an antispasmodic and excellent for coughs and bronchial conditions, as well as being a urinary cleanser. It has also been used for heartburn, a burning sensation below the ribcage. This suggests an aid in nervous conditions too.
Caution Very relaxing, so best avoided when needing to be alert.

Tea Tree*
Planet Saturn?
Botany The oil is distilled from the leaves of the melaleuca alternifolia tree.
Uses It has a strong antiseptic smell, and is probably a top note. Reputedly it has strong immuno-stimulant properties and apparently activates the white corpuscles to form a defence against invading organisms. It is helpful before and after operations for strengthening the body. It sweats out toxins and helps with infection generally, and is indicated for influenza and in cases of fever and exhaustion. A good all round cleansing oil, especially of the urinary tract.
Caution May cause skin irritation in people with sensitive skin.

Minerals

Understanding the history of a crystal, is entering the glory of God
'Esoteric Psychology', Alice Bailey, p.227

THE SUN
Alexandrite
No traditional planetary ruler. Its date of discovery in Russia saw the passing of the Sun and Moon through Taurus with its ruler, Venus, in a strong position in the heavens. However, the Russians associate it with the month of August, which may point to the Sun or Mercury.
Linked to the eyes.

Andalusite
Does not have a traditional planetary ruler but its yellow/red colour inclines it to the rulership of the Sun.
Linked to breaking with the past.

Chrysoberyl
No traditional planetary associations though may be linked to the Sun since crystals incline to a golden colour.
Linked to fertility problems.

Citrine
No traditional planetary rulership. Its colour and warmth suggests affiliation with the Sun.
Linked to joy, happiness and decision-making.

Cymophane
No known traditional association though modern writers link it to Venus and Jupiter, however its colour inclines it to the Sun.
Linked to eye disorders and balancing emotions.

Diamond
Both Al-Biruni and Ramesey say that diamond is ruled by Jupiter. But Ramesey also gives diamond to the Sun, as does Lilly under the name of adamant, another name for diamond, which seems likely as diamond disperses the light of the Sun. But then Lilly also gives diamond to Mars. Saturn may get a look in as diamond is a form of carbon which is ruled by this planet and Saturn also signifies anything that is hard, and diamond is the hardest substance known to man. Kunz says that diamond and other white stones are affiliated to the Moon. Gienger says that in many cultures diamond is

assigned to Venus, which is certainly true in Hindu astrology. Take your pick!
It is linked to illumination.

Garnet
Both Lilly and Ramesey say that the carbuncle is ruled by the Sun. Many red stones were once referred to as carbuncle. Nevertheless, the Sun does appear to be suitable since it rules the heart and circulation, the area which is associated with the red garnets.
It is linked to the circulation and reputedly helpful in anaemic states.

Gold
Both Lilly and Al-Biruni give gold to the Sun.
It is linked to protection, and has a reputation as a cure-all.

Helidor
Does not have a traditional planetary rulership but its name and colour incline it to the Sun.
It is linked to the lower chakras and the genital system.

Sodalite
No planetary rulership, though as is a constituent of the rock lapis lazuli it may show an influence of the Sun, Venus and Saturn, which according to astrological writers are connected to lapis. It is linked to the nervous system.

Spinel
No traditional rulership though the red spinel may be associated with the Sun or Mars.
It is linked to detoxification.

Sunstone
Obviously connected to the Sun through mythology, but no traditional rulerships appear to apply.
It is linked to the heart.

THE MOON
Amazonite
No traditional planetary associations but its mythology associates it with water and women, both ruled by the Moon. Its name of course refers to the possibly mythological Amazon warriors who bear a striking similarity to Diana, goddess of the hunt, the Moon, and childbirth. Its high copper

content may also suggest a Venus rulership.
It is linked to the reproductive system.

Apophyllite
No traditional planetary rulership, however, the clear variety may have a connection with the Moon. Also its water content suggests the Moon.
It is linked to divination and counselling.

Desert Rose
Selenite forms desert rose shapes when sea water evaporates. Selenite is connected to the Moon.
It is linked to releasing tension and activates creativity.

Fluorite
Does not appear to have a planetary ruler. Possibly connected to the Moon with its 'flowing' quality. Since its ingredient, fluoride, helps prevent tooth decay, it is possibly connected with Saturn, since that planet rules teeth.
It is linked to overcoming obstacles and water retention.

Herkimer Diamond
No actual planetary rulership is given but its connection to quartz and water gives an obvious choice of the Moon.
It is linked to releasing inhibitions, lifting depressed states, as well as toxic conditions.

Labradorite
No traditional planetary associations. There could be a link to the Moon with its changing sea-like colours.

Milky Quartz
No traditional planetary designation but most likely affiliated to the Moon since it is basically rock crystal with inclusions. Also because the Moon rules its white colour and the feminine aspect of personality.
It is linked to recovery from illness.

Moonstone
Al-Biruni, predictably, says this is ruled by the Moon. The Moon goddess Diana was linked to childbirth and the gestation.
It is also linked to the emotions, and female issues.

Opal
There does not appear to be a traditional planetary ruler but as it is a variety of quartz, so may have links with the Moon.
It is linked to alignment of the subtle bodies.

Pearl
Al-Biruni gives pearls to the Moon and Venus. Pearls have long been associated with the goddess Diana, the goddess of the Moon.
It is linked to feminine energy, giving a soothing and gentle effect.

Rock Crystal
Both Lilly and Al-Biruni say that the Moon rules rock crystal, which seems appropriate since the Moon rules white and anything colourless. It is linked to strong amplification of thought and memory.

Selenite
Due to its luminous white colour it is not surprising that Dariot, Lilly and Ramesay all say the Moon rules Selenite.
It is linked to telepathy and scrying.

Silver
Both Al-Biruni and Lilly give silver to the Moon. Its surface turns black parallel to the Moon's phases. Silver is associated with other Moon deities such as Isis, Selene and Diana.
It is linked to mind illumination.

MERCURY
Agate
Lilly gives the rulership to Mercury, and Ramesey concurs.
It is linked to the nervous system.

Amber
Al-Biruni says amber is ruled by Mercury. An 'androgynous stone' some say, which might be said of Mercury, (father of Hermaphrodite, of mixed sex), yet its colour seems to have kinship with the Sun.
It is linked to the nervous system and the heart.

Blue Lace Agate
Lilly and Ramesey give agate to Mercury, but it may also be influenced by Venus.
It is linked to throat problems.

Hematite
Lilly gives hematite's planetary rulership to Mercury and Saturn. Saturn is linked with black, the main colour of Hematite, so its rulership seems credible. Yet as an iron ore it suggests Mars.
It is linked to the blood circulation.

Jade
There is no traditional rulership in western astrology but jade is ruled by Mercury in Hindu astrology.
It is linked to healing the immune system.

Moss Agate
Agate is under the rulership of Mercury, according to Lilly and Ramesey, though moss agate may have a Saturn influence since the plant, moss, is under this planet.
It is linked to fertility.

Topaz
Dariot, Lilly and Ramesey give topaz to Mercury. But they also give it to Jupiter, and Ramesay gives it to the Sun. Michael Gienger states that most old cultures of Europe and India see topaz as a stone of Jupiter, although Imperial Topaz was given to the Sun. Therefore it has a mixed rulership of Mercury, the Sun and Jupiter, probably reflecting the various colours in which the crystal is found.
It is linked to a general healing quality.

Turquoise
Al-Biruni gives turquoise to Mercury.
It is linked to throat problems.

VENUS
Angelite
No traditional astrological associations. Although its connections to harmony may incline it to Venus, there seems a quality of Neptune about it due to the crystal's name and angelic associations.
It is linked to regeneration.

Aquamarine
A form of beryl, which Lilly ascribes to Venus. Sometimes it is linked to Neptune, god of the oceans, for obvious reasons.
It is linked to water retention.

Azurite
No traditional planetary association. Azure is an ore of copper (ruled by Venus) yet the colour azure is said to be ruled by Jupiter and Saturn according to Ramesey.
It is linked to the tendons.

Carnelian
Dariot and Lilly both agree on Venus as the ruler of carnelian.
It is linked to disorders of the blood.

Celestite
No traditional planetary affiliation though its folkloric associations seem to incline it to a Venus rulership. In astrology the sign of Libra is often said to be the 'iron fist in a velvet glove', which seems to describe the Celestite's gentle blue appearance masking the vibrant red strontium within.
It is linked to spiritual inspiration.

Chrysophrase
No traditional planetary associations. In antiquity it was apparently associated with Venus, the goddess of love.
It is linked to detoxification.

Copper
Dariot, Lilly and Ramesey all agree that Venus rules copper but Al-Biruni says Mars.
It is linked to rheumatism and arthritis.

Coral
Lilly connects coral with Venus.
It is linked to circulatory problems.

Dioptase
No traditional planetary rulership, but perhaps Venus due to its velvety green colour.
It is linked to heartache and unrequited love.

Dumortierite
No traditional planetary rulership, perhaps Venus or the Sun, since the colour pink is linked to love and the heart chakra.
It is linked to pain relief.

Emerald
Dariot, Lilly and Ramesey say Jupiter rules the emerald. However, Ramesey also says that Mercury and Venus are associated with it and Al-Biruni agrees with the latter but also includes the Moon. What confusion! Popularly emerald is assigned to Venus. although in the East, Mercury is assigned to it.
It is linked to the eyes, and as an all-healing stone.

Kyanite
No traditional planetary rulership, though could be linked with Venus due to its colour.
It is linked to tonic action on the glands.

Malachite
Not specified traditionally, but could be Venus due to malachite's copper content, copper being a metal of Venus.
It is linked to restoring equilibrium.

Marcasite
Lilly says the planetary rulership belongs to Venus but also gives the rulership to Mercury. Cornel gives marcasite to the Moon. So take your pick.
It is linked to hurts from the past.

Peridot
No traditional planetary rulership, however, Crysolite, a less intense green form of peridot which is ruled by Venus and the Sun according to Dariot, Lilly and Ramesay, is linked to the heart chakra, therefore, suggestive of love, both personal and universal.

Rhodochrosite
No traditional planetary rulership.
It is linked to the emotions and mentality.

Rose Quartz
No given planetary rulership but Lilly gives Venus to the rose flower and Venus exemplifies many of the qualities associated with rose quartz, such as love, peace and harmony. It has been suggested as good for tissue regeneration in the kidneys, the part of the body ruled by Venus.
It is linked to the heart, physically and emotionally.

Sapphire
Dariot, Lilly and Ramesay say that the sapphire belongs to Venus as well as Saturn. Lilly and Ramesay also give the sapphire to Jupiter. Venus may

score over the other planets as the colour blue is associated with Venus. However, the very dark blue, almost black sapphires may be associated with Saturn, black being Saturn's colour.
It is linked to throat and eye problems.

Tourmaline
According to Arabic traditions, tourmaline is a stone of the Sun strengthening the heart and protecting from nightmares.
It is linked to healing or aligning the subtle bodies.

Unakite
No traditional planetary association but its combined colours of pink and green suggest the heart chakra and love. Possibly of Venus rulership.
It is linked to the heart and emotions.

MARS
Bloodstone
Both Lilly and Ramesey agree on Mars ruling the bloodstone, but under its other name of heliotrope. Ramesey also says the Sun rules it. The word 'helios' is Greek for the Sun. Both the Sun and Mars are connected to the blood.
It is linked to the circulation.

Iron
It is generally agreed by astrologers that Mars rules iron.
It is linked to the blood circulation.

Jasper
Dariot, Lilly and Ramesey agree on Mars. They may have red jasper in mind since green jasper is apparently ruled by Venus, according to Ramesey.
It is linked to kidney problems.

Magnetite (Lodestone)
Dariot and Lilly both say Mars and Saturn rule it and they call it lodestone.
It is linked to searching for guidance.

Pyrite
No traditional rulership, but sulphur of which pyrite is an important source, is also known as 'brimstone' which Lilly assigns to the rulership of Mars. Pyrite's high iron content may indeed be appropriate to the rulership of the fiery Mars.
It is linked to creating a strong energy field.

Tiger's Eye
No known planetary rulership but its iron oxide inclusions incline it to the rulership of Mars (which rules iron).
It is linked to stabilising the lower chakras.

JUPITER
Calcite
No traditional rulership, but calcite belongs to the calc-silicates group of rocks closely related to marble, and marble is traditionally ruled by Jupiter, but may also be linked to Saturn, for calcium.
It is linked to bladder problems.

Charoite
Does not have a traditional planetary rulership, though its purple colour may link it to Jupiter.
It is linked to the immune system.

Iolite
No traditional planetary rulership though its purple colour may associate it with Jupiter.
It is linked to clairvoyant abilities.

Kunzite
Its modern discovery means it has no traditional planetary rulership, though its colour inclines it to Jupiter, or perhaps Venus.
It is linked to flow of the life force.

Lepidolite
No traditional planetary rulership but possibly Jupiter due to its purple colour.
It links to periods of calm, peace and relaxation.

Tanzanite
No traditional planetary rulership, but apparently the American Gem Trade Association have made it an "official" birthstone for the month of December.
It is linked to low back pain.

Thulite
Its colour purple is linked to Jupiter, but there is no traditional rulership.
It is linked to regenerating the aura.

Tin
Astrologers all agree that Jupiter rules tin. Interestingly any tin absorbed by humans usually collects in the liver, also ruled by Jupiter, as well as the skeleton, though it is not an essential mineral for the body.
It is linked to protection.

SATURN
Aragonite
No traditional rulership. Since Aragonite makes up the shell of sea-creatures, its connection with water might suggest a Moon rulership. But calcium in the hard skeleton may also suggest a Saturn rulership.
It is linked to problems with the skeletal system.

Jet
All black stones are collectively ruled by Saturn, says Lilly.
It is linked to calmness and tranquillity.

Lapis Lazuli
Dariot, Lilly and Ramesey say Saturn, but Lilly and Ramesey also say Venus; Al-Biruni thinks the Sun rules lapis.
It links to alleviating depression.

Lead
Al-Biruni, Dariot, Lilly and Ramesey all say Saturn rules lead.
It links to protection and defence.

Obsidian
Since Lilly remarks that all black stones belong to Saturn, by association obsidian belongs to Saturn. Modern thought has also connected obsidian with Pluto.
It is linked to creating structure in life, possibly DNA.

Onyx
No traditional rulership but onyx may be connected to the planet Saturn, which rules black, the main colour of onyx.
It is linked to calming the emotions and hearing.

Petrified Wood
No traditional planetary rulership, though it has strong links with the planet Earth.
It is linked to rheumatic conditions.

Smoky Quartz
No traditional planetary affiliations, though the black variety may be linked to Saturn.

THE OUTER PLANETS
Tektites
No traditional astrological rulership, but its other-worldly nature seems to align it with the outer planets, Uranus, Neptune and Pluto. Tektite may have an ability to align the subtle bodies, since these three planets are associated with them. Uranus with the etheric body, Neptune with the emotional body and Pluto with the mental body.
It is linked to aura healing.

References

1. CA, p.71.
2. ibid, p.257
3. Tisserand R. *Aromatherapy for Everyone*, Arkana, 1990, p.69.
4. Passebecq L. *Aromatherapy*, p.155.
5. CH, p.101.
6. ibid p.155.
7. CA, p.82.
8. CA. p.79.
9. CH, p.73.
10. CA, p.75.
11. Hoare J. *The Complete Aromatherapy Tutor*, Gaia Books Ltd, 2010, p.94.
12. CH, p.188.
13. CA. p.71.
14. Berg A. 'Vitex Agnus-castus', *Aromatherapy Times Spring* 2010.
15. ibid.
16. CA. p.63.
17. CA. p.59.

18

Steps to Judgement

There are more diseases that terminate in health than in death
'Christian Astrology', William Lilly, p.291

Consideration and Judgement

1. Check planetary hour of decumbiture. Is it significant in the judgement?

2. Compare the strength of the Fortunes and Infortunes.

3. Calculate the strength of the Ascendant ruler, the Sun, Moon and Mercury in order to ascertain the strength of the constitution, the heart, general bodily function, and the flow of the Vital Spirits, respectively.

4. Examine the 1st house.
   a) Aspects from planets to the Ascending degree
   b) The planetary ruler of the 1st house
   c) Planets positioned in the 1st house
   d) Planets positioned in the 1st house/different sign

5. Examine the sign on the 6th house cusp.
   a) Aspects from planets to the cusp of 6th house
   b) The planetary ruler of the 6th house
   c) Planets positioned in the 6th house
   d) Compare strength of 1st and 6th house rulers

6. Judge how far the physician (therapist/astrologer/healer), can effect a cure by examining the 7th house.

7. Note any planetary links from the 1st house to those of the 4th, 8th and 12th houses.

8. Examine the efficacy of possible treatment/medicines signified by the 10th house.

9. Check if the Moon is Void of Course.

10. Check for besiegement of significant planets.

11. Check reception between planets.

12. Check for Fixed Stars, Azimene Degrees, Antiscia, Arabic Parts, Midpoints.

13. Timing and length of disease.
    a) Monitor planets for change of sign, house, and whether they turn direct, stationary, or retrograde
    b) Moon for acute diseases, Sun for chronic diseases

Note: It is important to observe the movement of planets in the decumbiture chart since certain factors may occur to prevent aspects perfecting. These include Prohibition, Frustration and Refranation

Prohibition
If two planets are applying to one another but another planet intercepts before the original aspect can be completed this makes the original aspect ineffectual.

Frustration
This is similar to Prohibition in that a faster moving planet like Mercury at 5 degrees Libra is trying to reach the conjunction of Venus at 10 Libra, but before this aspect can be perfected, Venus completes a square with Saturn at 11 degrees Capricorn.

Refranation
Two planets may be applying to one another but before they can perfect an aspect, one of them turns retrograde.

Given overleaf is a grid which may be helpful to structure the position of the planets.

Planetary Dignity and Debility

	SATURN Cold & Dry	JUPITER Hot & Moist	MARS Hot & Dry	SUN Hot & Dry	VENUS Cold & Moist	MERCURY Cold & Dry	MOON Cold & Moist
SIGN/ HUMOUR							
DIGNITIES Reception							
DEBILITIES Detriment Fall Peregrine							
BESEIGEMENT Fortunes/ Infortunes COMBUSTION							
HOUSES Angular Succedent Cadent Joy							
MOTION Fast/Slow Stationary Retrograde							
FIXED STARS							
AZIMENE							
ANTISCIA							
ARABIC PARTS							

130   Introduction to Decumbiture

MIDPOINTS							
HAYZ							
DEG. NODES SZYZGY							

A helpful grid to determine the movement of the Moon follows on the next page.

This is Cardan's* Decumbiture relating to one John Baptista Triandule, a gentleman from Verona, Italy.

Decumbiture Chart: Cardan's Decumbiture[1]
3 November 1581, 21:16 hrs (9.16 pm), Padua, Italy, 45N24 11E53

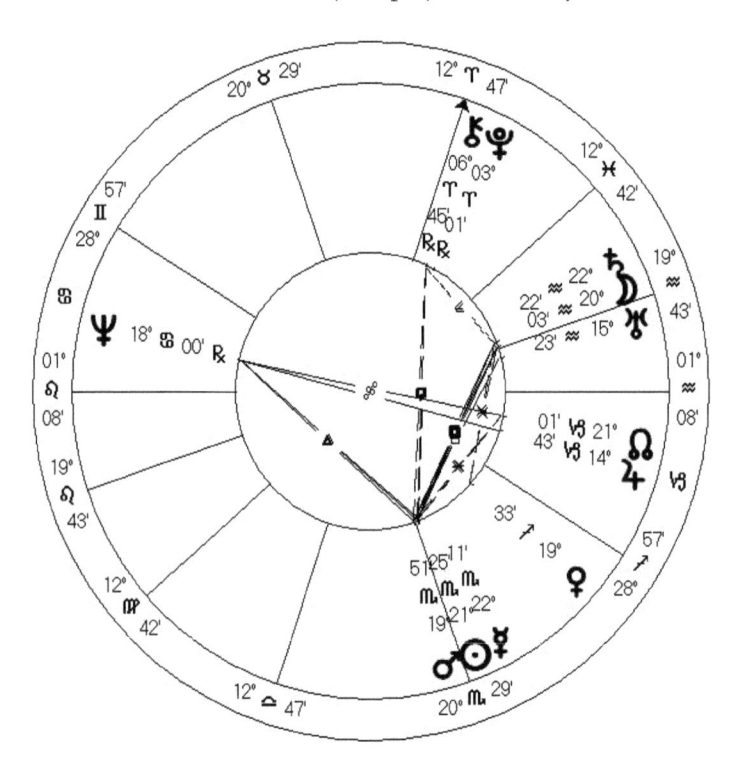

Steps to Judgement   131

Transit of Moon

Decumbiture: Data:

0	1	2	3	4	5	6	7	8	9	10	11	12	13	14	15	16	17	18	19	20	21	22	23	24	25	26	27	28	29	30	31

Transit of Moon

Decumbiture: Sword Wound   Data: 3rd Nov 1581, 21:16, Padua, Italy

0	1	2	3	4	5	6	7	8	9	10	11	12	13	14	15	16	17	18	19	20	21	22	23	24	25	26	27	28	29	30	31
AC ♌		♀ ♈										MC ♈		♂ ♐	♅ ♒		♆ ♏	☊ ♏	☽ ♒	☉ ♏	☿ ♏										
																		♀	♐		♃ ♒	♄ ♒										

The young man suffered a sword injury to his knee during his studentship in Padua. The injury unfortunately resulted in the amputation of his whole leg. It is an understatement to say that the wound was a grievous one, but it was so, and the physicians did despair of the man's life. Not withstanding their fears, he recovered and lived for two more years going 'upon a wooden leg'.[2]

The house cusps coincide with a Topocentric house system. With the Part of Death at 0.48 Leo in the area of the Ascendant, the situation looks dire from the start. The Ascendant however, varies about a degree from the chart in Culpeper's book, doubtless owing to computerisation. Culpeper has 28 Cancer rising, and our chart has 1 Leo. However, Culpeper himself states that it matters not whether it is the Sun or the Moon ruling the Ascendant in this chart since both are afflicted and indicative of weakness on the part of the patient.

The following is to illustrate the use of the grid for the dignities and debilities of the planets.

Name John Baptista Triandule
Planetary Dignity and Debility

	SATURN Cold & Dry	JUPITER Hot & Moist	MARS Hot & Dry	SUN Hot & Dry	VENUS Cold & Moist	MERCURY Cold & Dry	MOON Cold & Moist
SIGN/ HUMOUR	Aquarius Hot & Moist	Capricorn Cold & Dry	Scorpio Cold & Moist	Scorpio Cold & Moist	Sagittarius Hot & Dry	Scorpio Cold & Moist	Aquarius Hot & Moist
DIGNITIES Reception	Domicile	Term	Domicile			Term Exchange Trip with Moon	Face Exchange Trip with Mercury
DEBILITIES Detriment Fall Peregrine		Fall		Peregrine	Peregrine		
BESIEGEMENT Fortunes Infortunes COMBUSTION			Combust			Combust	
HOUSES Angular Succedent Cadent Joy	Succedent	Cadent	Succedent	Succedent	Succedent Joy	Succedent	Succedent

MOTION Fast/Slow Stationary Retrograde	Fast	Slow	Slow	Slow	Slow	Slow	Slow
FIXED STARS							
AZIMENE			Azimene		Azimene		
ANTISCIA							
ARABIC PARTS							
MIDPOINTS					Mars/ Jupiter Mars/ Neptune Saturn/ Neptune		
HAYZ					Below Earth	Below Earth	
DEG. NODES SZYZGY							

Incidentally, if the degree of the Ascendant is a very late one, and another sign takes up most of the 1st house, then rulers of both signs should be judged in respect of the constitution.[3]

It would seem that the Moon does have some strength since it is in reception by triplicity with Mercury and in its own face, yet it is overshadowed by its conjunction to a strong Saturn in Aquarius, who is fast in motion. The Lord of Death also rules the 8th house of death, which bodes ill.

The Sun ruling Leo fares no better, since it is peregrine, conjunct a strong Mars in Scorpio. That Mars is on an azimene degree describes, it would seem, the piercing sword wound.

Therefore, both the Moon and the Sun, are conjunct two strong malefics, which is not very promising for continuance of the vital spirits. Further, the Moon is square Mars, and the Sun square Saturn. An unpromising judgement it would seem. Planets are often a combination of both strong and weak factors.[4] No doubt therein lies the art!

Yet despite the dire situation, the young man recovered. Culpeper put this down to help from the Fortunes: Venus sextile the Moon and Jupiter sextile the Sun. It matters not, it would appear, that the aspects are separating ones. The orbs allowed between planets are greater in traditional astrology. Venus is not particularly a strong Fortune, since she is peregrine and on azimene degree, but it seems to matter not. Venus ruling 4th house shows a good end to the matter, though in this case Venus is a mixed blessing where midpoints are concerned. Venus is on Mars/Jupiter which is protective of health, but also on the Mars/Neptune midpoint which threatens infection and Saturn/Neptune midpoint which creates organic imbalance. Since Venus is in Sagittarius ruling legs, it is possible that the weak condition of the young man's stump became infected.

Jupiter, which rules the 6th house, is placed in intercepted Capricorn in the 6th indicating the area of affliction, the knee. In detriment it shows the knee to be in a poor state, but the North Node, a benefic close by, is another pointer for resumption of health.

The strength of the Infortunes may also be conducive to the strength of the physician's physic, since they rule the 7th and 10th respectively.

Both Lilly and Culpeper are always at pains to point out in their writings that no matter how ominous a situation may look, the intervening aspects of the Fortunes will often help the sick to recover. Their timely intervention mitigates the force of the malefics, it would seem. The young man rallied, albeit for just another two years. It is interesting that there is a two-degree difference between Mars and Sun, Moon and Saturn, and there are two degrees before the end of Sagittarius, the sign on the 6th house cusp. Fixed planets where the Lights are placed are also counted in years.

References

1. CH, p.130.
2. ibid p.131
3. BI, p.279.
4. BI, p.316.

19

Case Histories

A physician without astrology is like a pudding without fat.
'Astrological Judgement of Diseases from the Decumbiture of the Sick',
N. Culpeper, p.69

Decumbiture: Painful Big Toe
2 February 2013 14:00 51N58 0E35

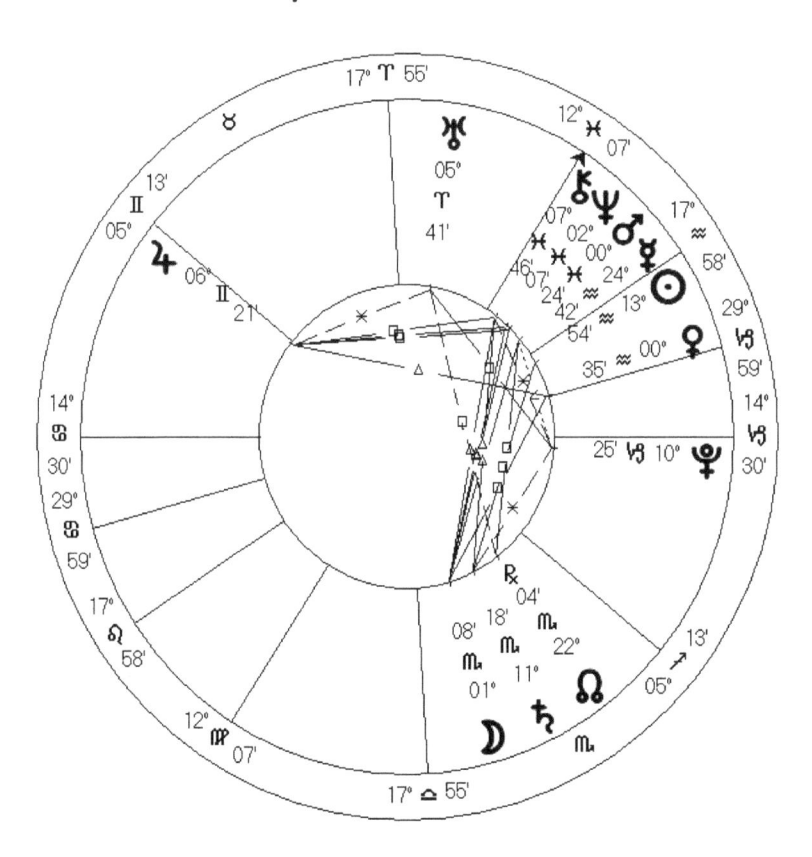

Background
The patient, a lady in her eighties, had been looking for answers from her orthodox physicians, but after certain tests no cause could be determined for the pain in her right toe. Gout had been ruled out. The time is taken for a reflexology appointment, as she intuitively felt this therapy might be of help.

In reflexology, the big toe reflects the head and all its structures like the brain, nervous system and endocrine system.

Astrology
Cancer, a Water sign, linked to fluids, rises with its ruler the Moon in Scorpio, elimination. The Moon in detriment and peregrine shows weakness. In the 5th house, the heart and kidneys come under focus. According to Lilly's Table of Further Considerations (Chapter 9), this also pinpoints the head, breast and stomach, echoing the Cancer Ascendant. Unfortunately the Moon is applying to the Part of Sickness at 3°36' Scorpio, which is not helpful.

The Moon's last aspect was a square to Venus in Aquarius in the 8th, which appeared problematical where circulation and elimination was concerned. The fact that the next aspect was a conjunction to Saturn did not bode well, especially as Saturn rules both the 7th and 8th houses. But since Saturn also rules the 9th house of good fortune, there could be ameliorating factors. Nevertheless, an application to Saturn could only mean a protracted condition.

Sickness
Once the case history was taken it became apparent that Sagittarius on the 6th house cusp was appropriate as the patient had a history of leg problems. She had an operation on her left leg some years ago for cancer of the skin, and it was prone to swelling, most probably oedema. Indeed, she had bursitis, a swelling due to collection of fluids. The Cancer Ascendant becomes meaningful.

Sagittarius, a mutable sign, indicates that the condition may come and go and the patient agreed that the pain does fluctuate. The ruler of 6th, Jupiter, in Gemini in the 12th house, describes the nervous system and the feet, as well as the immune system. It turned out that the patient had an operation on a trapped nerve, also a number of years ago, on her right foot! It had been a very serious operation which had left her leg very swollen.

Jupiter also rules the 10th house of medicine, which might point to the operation being culprit, to some extent. Chiron on the cusp of the 10th, square Jupiter, seems to confirm that some treatment may be linked to the present condition.

Jupiter is in detriment and therefore weak, but gains strength by exchanging term with Mercury, and is in his own face. This makes the 'condition' marginally stronger than the patient, and would mean a hard road to some sort of relief. Would it get worse before it got better? That is what often happens with complementary therapies, known as the 'healing response'.

Certainly with Mars in Pisces in an applying square to Jupiter, it threatened inflammation, but fortunately cool Venus perfected the trine to Jupiter beforehand, so it appeared as if that calamity would be averted.

In summary it appeared as if the patient was weak, with low immunity and the possibility of problems with her nervous system.

Treatment

During reflexology treatment, sensitive areas obviously included the right big toe. The left one also was a little painful. Other areas of sensitivity were the middle spine on both feet, and just under the diaphragm on both feet. Treatment included reflexology on both feet finishing with a massage with peppermint essential oil in a carrier oil.

Peppermint was chosen for its cooling and balancing nature, the medication in accordance with the nature of the Lord of the Ascendant as suggested by Culpeper. Cancer is cold and moist, the Moon its ruler is cold and moist, the position in Scorpio is cold and moist, and antipathetical to the Lord of the 6th, Sagittarius, which is hot and moist. Peppermint is ruled by Venus, which was applying to Jupiter, ruling the condition. The ruler of the 10th house, which designates medicines, is Jupiter and that is afflicted, so Jupiter-ruled medicines are not advised. Immediate results were positive, with less pain.

First 'Crisis'

An appointment for the following week 9th February 2013 coincided with the first crisis day when the Moon would be square to itself. The patient reported that her healing response to the last treatment resulted in an overwhelming tiredness which itself resulted in the best night's sleep she had had for a long time. The pain in her toe had lessened as well, but by the next appointment the situation remained intermittent. However, the transit Moon in Aquarius was moving to a trine of natal Jupiter so the situation looked hopeful. The treatment was never wholly successful but it made the pain less acute and more bearable.

Decumbiture: Post Operative Weakness
2 March 2011 21:10 51N58 000E35

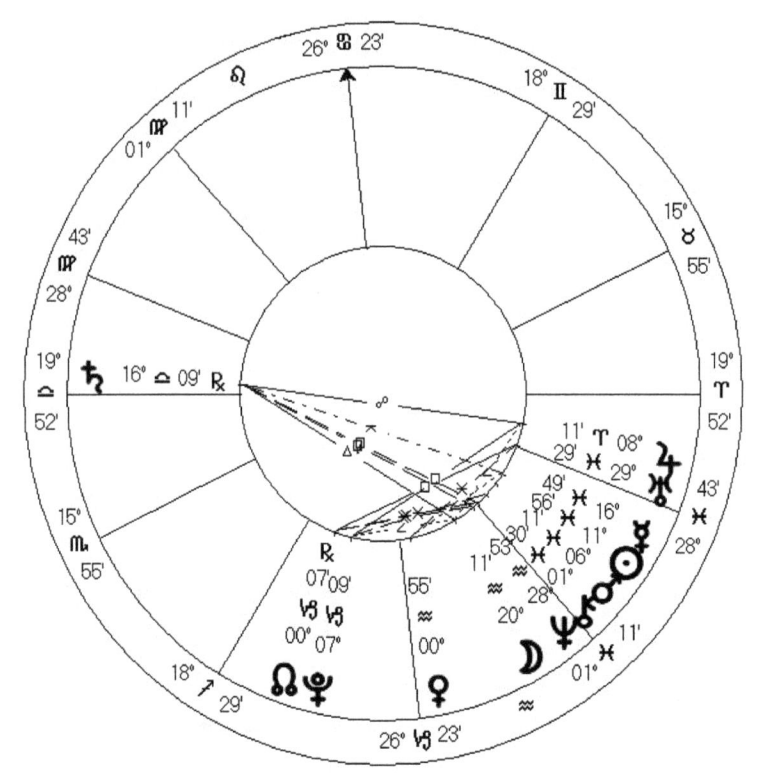

Background and Consultation

A client scheduled for a reiki treatment to re-balance her energies after an operation on her knee to repair damage caused by arthritis. At the same time she asked me if I could recommend essential oils for the scar on her knee resulting from the operation.

During reiki treatment the energy around the knees felt extremely hot, whereas around the calves and feet it felt very cold. After treatment, the client asked if I had felt any change of energy around the womb area; I had not. The client said she actually had spotting in between periods and after intimate relations. The client was menopausal age. She was waiting for the results of tests, and feared the worst.

Libra is rising; the sign of the balance and the object of the reiki treatment. The planets are generally below the horizon so the condition is obscure: indeed she is seeking answers for her symptoms.

Venus, the ruler of Ascendant, is cold and moist and is in Aquarius, hot and moist, so she is feeling uncomfortable, as revealed in the reiki treatment. The circulation and calves are under consideration since Venus is in Aquarius.

Venus is in the 4th house, angular and strong, but something is coming to an end. Since Venus rules the womb, and the 8th house, it shows the reproductive system. It may describe the end of her child-bearing years. Venus has an applying sextile to Jupiter, the ruler of the 6th house, which is helpful.

But Venus is in mutual reception with Saturn on the Ascendant, retrograde, which is not particularly good since it rules the 4th house, the end of the matter. Things could take a long time to get back to normal. Saturn is strong by exaltation and face, and rules the bones and knees. There was restriction on her walking.

Pisces on the 6th cusp in a late degree, suggests that the situation has been around for some time. Jupiter in Aries in the 6th, its own triplicity, is about equal in strength with Venus. The situation looks like a difficult one because Jupiter appears to be applying to an opposition of Saturn, which really looked as if the client would have bad news regarding the bleeding, and problems with arthritis, since Jupiter rules the arterial circulation and Saturn the bones.

But the sextile of Venus to Jupiter will perfect before Jupiter arrives at the opposition to Saturn. Further, Jupiter is in mutual reception with Mars, which rules the 7th house of the physician, so physicians are able to help.

Within a few days the client told me that results had come in showing nothing serious, i.e. cancer, but she was waiting for more tests to see exactly what the problem might be.

Physic

Cancer is on the cusp of the 10th house of medicine. Its ruler the Moon is in its own face, not too strong, and the Moon is also void of course with an exact trine to the Ascendant. The Ascendant changes every four minutes, so it is suggestive of cooling medicine.

Moon-ruled essential oils are scarce, and the only one reputedly helpful for the womb is Clary Sage, so that could be a consideration. But a tonic to circulation to rebalance the hot/cold energies was needed, and I decided on a Saturn-ruled essential oil, as Saturn is the dispositor of both the Moon and Venus, representative of the client. The Moon was separating from a trine of Saturn and heading for the Ascendant so Cypress, a Saturn-ruled essential oil would also be good for circulation, scarring and heavy menstruation.

Culpeper always suggests strengthening the heart if the Sun is weak, and in this chart the Sun is peregrine. I chose Neroli (from the Orange tree), which is not so much a tonic but it soothes the heart and is helpful for new skin growth. Lemon sun oil is good for circulation and is a tonic for the heart and the immune system. Lemon might also help with constipation. The client reported that the scarring had greatly improved within a few months and continued doing so.

Decumbiture: Collision with Fork Left Truck
19 June 2007 18:10 52N40 1E15

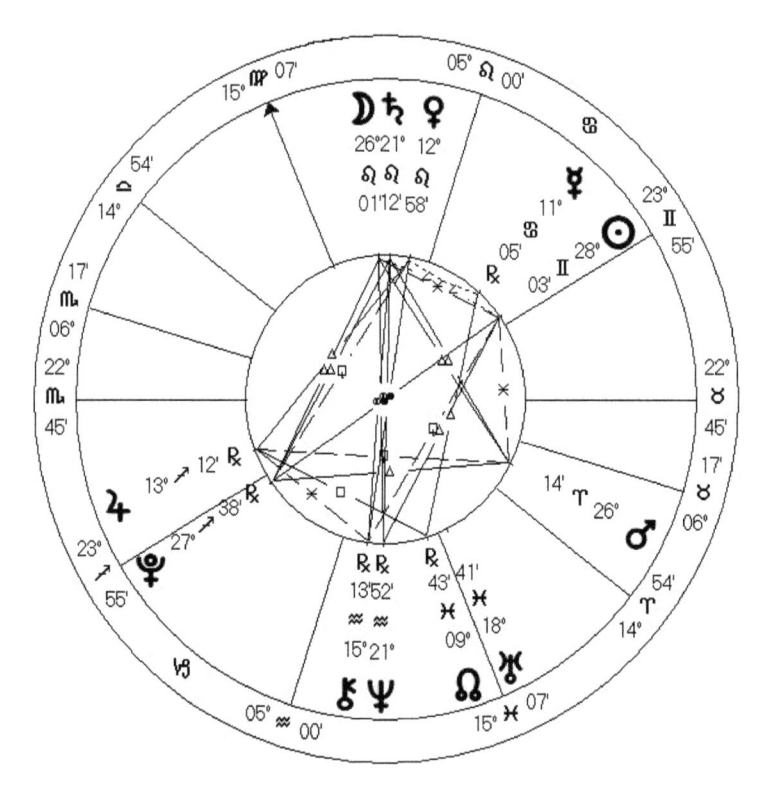

Background

The patient had been working at the back of a trailer, checking that it was sealed, when he was knocked to the floor by a forklift truck (a powered truck that lifts and transports goods) and his right leg got caught under the forks, dragging him along. The forklift was being driven forward with the view blocked by a higher than normal pallet when the truck should have been driven in reverse using mirrors.

Only by the patient shouting at the top of his voice was the driver alerted of the incident. The patient was convinced that his leg would have been severely crushed had the driver not stopped. Nevertheless, besides cuts and bruising, he did suffer a severe sprain which had him hobbling about for three weeks.

The two GPs he consulted were unable to help him, and in the opinion of the patient, quite useless. One said he could return to work on the Monday after the accident, even though he could barely walk and certainly could not drive. The other grabbed hold of his leg touching the wound causing him to howl with embarrassment.

A McTimoney chiropractor (using a method of adjusting bones to improve alignment of skeleton and help nervous system to work more efficiently) the patient had visited before, was able to treat him and bring him back to a good state of health. The scarring has disappeared but the patient still gets flashbacks.

Astrology
The Scorpio Ascendant can be indicative of a challenging situation, but Mars the ruler is resilient in its domicile, Aries. A masculine sign shows the right side of the body where the injury was sustained.

The Injury
Taurus on the 6th cusp in an early degree suggests a recent matter. Venus the ruler, cold and moist, is in hot and dry Leo, peregrine, cadent, and therefore weaker than Mars, so the patient is stronger than the injury. In the 9th it describes 'transport'. Venus is also ruler of the hour, a protective influence normally, but interestingly conjunct the Part of Catastrophe.

The injury is aptly described by the movement of the Moon which translates Saturn by conjunction to Mars by an applying trine. Saturn, a heavy planet, describes heavy equipment that may be faulty since Saturn is in detriment. Saturn is fittingly on the Mars/Uranus midpoint of accidents, also involving Neptune which may account for the flashbacks.

Healing
Healing occurs through the auspices of physicians and their medications. This is quite weak in this case because a weak Venus also rules the 7th, indicating that help is not at hand. Not in the guise of the first two GPs evidently.

Their medicine is not helpful either since Mercury which rules the 10th house has little strength. It exchanges face with the Sun, but any strength is demolished by being retrograde and on an azimene degree. Further, it is in the 8th house of toxicity.

Yet no matter the state of Venus, it is in an applying trine to Jupiter, the Greater Fortune, indicating that there is a strong possibility of healing, especially since Jupiter in Sagittarius describes the legs, the injured area. Jupiter in the 1st house usually helps strengthen the constitution, though its retrograde motion indicates healing will take some time. The fact that the situation will end well is shown through Jupiter's rulership of the 4th house – the end of the matter.

Decumbiture: Shaky Legs
30 September 2010 13:28 51N58 000E35

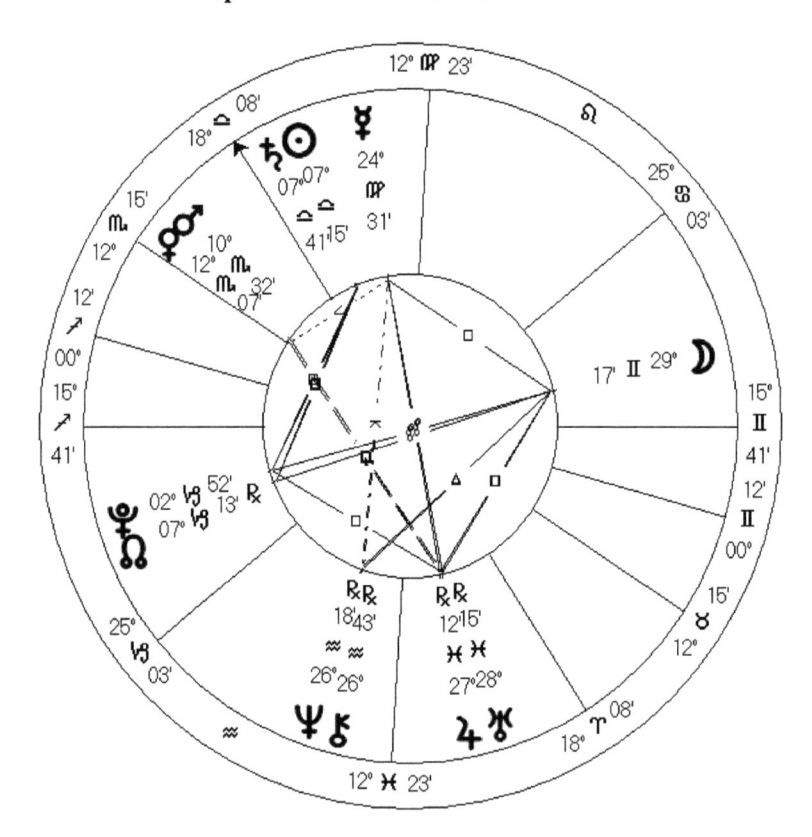

Background
The patient's state of health was linked to other matters. What they were was revealed during a consultation chart reading.

Client
Sagittarius on the Ascendant and the 12th house cusp indicates restriction of some kind, possibly hospitalisation. The Part of Fatality on the Ascendant looks ominous for the client. Sagittarius rules the legs, Jupiter in Pisces

rules the feet and its retrograde motion suggests restriction again. Difficult to ignore is Jupiter's conjunction to Uranus, which indicates some spasmodic motion. At this point the client revealed that she had been in hospital for some time and that now she was very shaky on her legs. The client said she was greatly incapacitated due to illness.

Illness
Indeed, Jupiter signifying the client is opposing Mercury, the 6th house ruler, signifying illness. Mercury in Virgo suggests digestive problems, particularly the intestines. It turned out that she had had five operations for hernia, a protrusion of the intestine through a weak part of the abdominal wall. Unfortunately, Mercury ruling the disease is very strong in this chart by domicile, exaltation and face, so the client's illness is difficult to overcome.

Crises
Some crisis seems to have occurred since the Moon, which rules the 8th house, is in a separating square from both Mercury and Jupiter. The Moon is in the 7th, Mercury also rules the 7th, as well as the 6th of course, so the crisis involves patient and physicians. Mercury also ruling the 9th house possibly indicates a legal dispute.

The client revealed she was in a legal dispute with the hospital and physicians over the operations which left her incapacitated. The client said she could no longer work. Venus ruling the 10th of career, and medicine, is in detriment in Scorpio and conjunct Mars ruling the 4th house, the end of the matter. The combination of the MC on the Mars/Uranus midpoint of operations, and the fixed star Acrux on its ruler, Venus, suggest benefits linked to health.

Naturally the client wanted to know the outcome of the lawsuit. Would she win damages? Both the client and the opposing party are shown by Jupiter and Mercury ruling the 1st and 7th respectively. They are strong in their own signs, and Mercury's essential dignity is stronger by exaltation and own face. Both planets are weakened by being slow in motion, Jupiter further weakened by being retrograde, and in a cadent house. So far Mercury appears stronger.

Coming to the Plaintiff's aid however, is the benefic North Node in the 1st house, with a strong dispositor, Saturn in exaltation in Libra. This means that the South Node is in the Defendant's house. Unfortunately for the Plaintiff, the dispositor is Mercury and very strong.

My feeling was that the client would be awarded some damages but not as much as she had hoped, which proved to be the case.

Decumbiture: Knot in Solar Plexus
21 NOVEMBER 2012 51N58 000E35

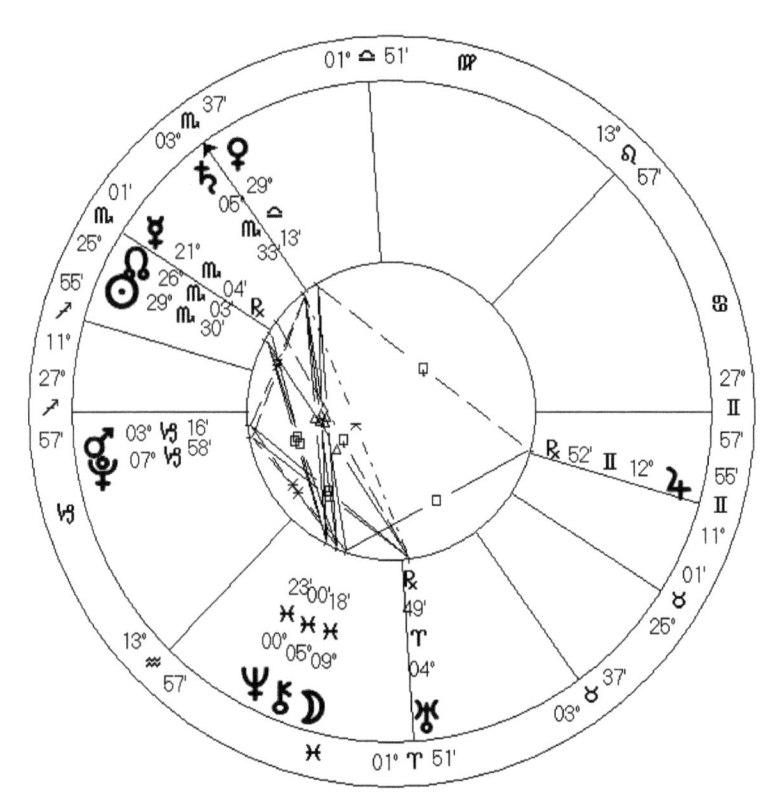

Background

Michael complained of a tight knot in the area of his solar plexus chakra (centre of diaphragm), which seemed to interfere with his breathing. This suggested a sluggish flow of oxygen, and a resulting tiredness, which he confirmed.

He had been experiencing panic attacks over the last few years which he had learnt to control through meditation. He had booked a crystal healing session since he intuitively felt that this might help him. Crystal healing appears to work on the subtle bodies and meridians of the body, basically by putting them into balance. Crystals are chosen intuitively, colour and shape play a large part, as well as various anecdotal and folkloric evidence.

Initially, it felt as if crystals of a relaxing nature and colour would be most suitable, but the colour red suggested itself, which I immediately rejected as I felt that crystals of that colour would be too 'harsh'. I set up a decumbiture chart to see if it might give guidance, particularly in relation to the choice of crystals.

Constitution

The Sagittarius Ascendant in a late degree suggests that the condition might be at an end. Sagittarius/Gemini across the horizon links into the respiratory as well as the nervous system. Aspects to the Ascendant include a strong Venus, domicile, angular and fast in motion, in sextile, which is helpful for the constitution and choice of medicines as it is on the cusp of the 10th house.

Nevertheless, the Ascendant-ruler Jupiter is in a poor condition, in detriment in Gemini and retrograde, though not entirely without dignity since Jupiter is in its own term. It is hot and moist and so is Gemini. This suggests that the patient is not totally overwhelmed by his condition, but the mutable Gemini indicates that the condition is a fluctuating one. Being in the 6th house, it is not a good sign for the patient.

Jupiter is linked to the lungs in Gemini, which describes the client's slight breathing problems. In the table 'Members in Man's Body', Jupiter in Gemini signifies 'breast, kidneys and genitals'. It is in the area of the breast, loosely speaking, where Michael experienced feelings of pressure.

Illness

Mercury, the ruler of the 6th house, disposes Jupiter. Mercury is said to be basically cold and dry and is in Scorpio, a cold and moist sign. So comparing Jupiter and Mercury we have extremes of temperature. Mercury is not particularly strong being retrograde - describing the sluggish flow of breath - though it is in its own term. Unfortunately, Mercury also rules the 7th house, so the 'physician' does not appear to have the greatest power to help.

Medicine

The 10th house looks more promising although initially with the position of Saturn therein, it does not look as if that might be the case. However, Saturn is dignified by reception with Mars and triplicity exchange with Venus, as well as being conjunct the latter Fortune and good aspects generally. Above the Earth in a diurnal chart, Saturn is in his correct hayz. Saturn's rulership of Capricorn, intercepted in the 1st house, influences the patient's constitution. It has repressed strength one might say.

Mars rules the 10th house and is extremely strong through exaltation and reception with Saturn, exchanging term with Venus and face with Jupiter, and angular. A sextile to Saturn is the most helpful aspect.

It would appear that the Infortunes are stronger in this chart than the Fortunes, which indicates a more difficult path towards health. Nevertheless, even though Mars is a malefic, it is dignified and therefore the medicines - in this case crystals - may be effective. Indeed, dignified Infortunes may on occasion, actually help.[1] Mars rules the colour red, confirming my own intuitive selection. It would appear that the patient needed the energy of Mars, since it appeared that this was lacking in his constitution.

Nevertheless, I opted for a softer colour and chose pink crystals, that is Rose Quartz, to place on the chakras, particularly as Venus is conjunct the MC. I actually did not place a crystal on the solar plexus chakra as I felt it needed to 'breathe' so placed crystals either side, on the heart and sacral chakras. Grounding crystals chosen were Haematite, made up of oxygen and iron chemicals, the latter ruled by Mars.

Transit of the Moon
The Moon is cold and moist and in Pisces, itself cold and moist. Its last separating aspect was a trine to a strong Saturn and the next applies by square to a relatively weak Jupiter and the 6th house cusp. This may indicate a catharsis, that the client may feel worse before he gets better or an over-active healing response.

Result
Immediately after the treatment, the client felt that the knot had dispersed.

Decumbiture: Infertility
18 October 2010 10.00 35N27 139E39

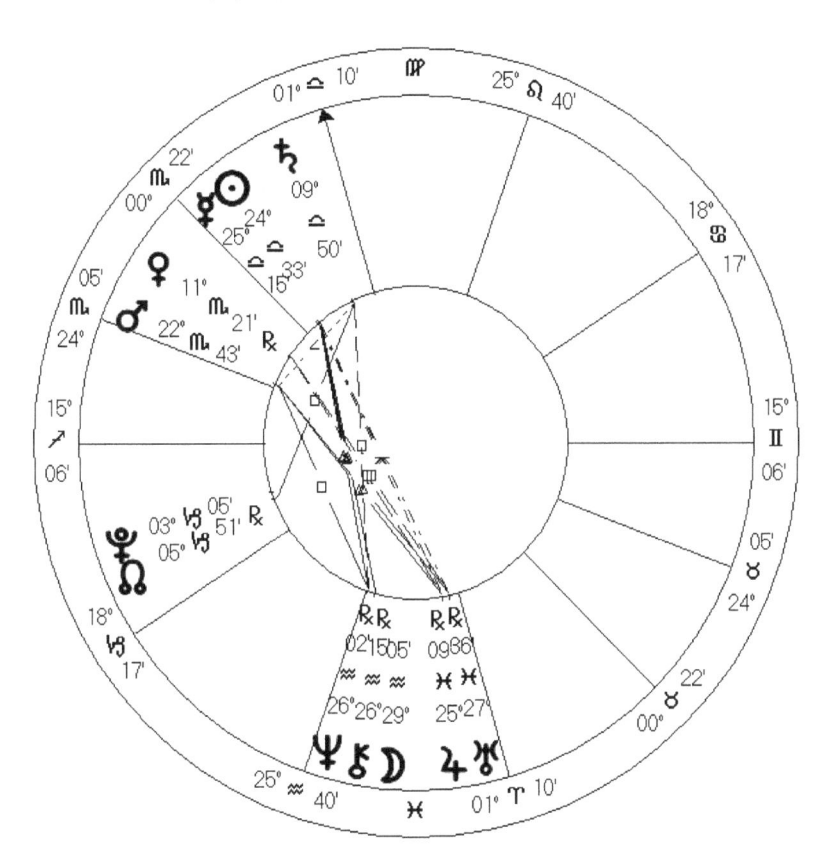

Background

This was a decumbiture handed to me of an appointment at a clinic, without giving me the reason for the appointment. The client was obviously in a difficult situation, notwithstanding her significator, Jupiter, appearing strong in domicile. It is retrograde and in an intercepted sign, the 3rd, indicating oppression of the mind.

Her health condition is shown by Venus, ruler of the 6th, as well as the 5th, hinting at the problem being one concerning children. A problem obviously exists since Venus is in detriment in Scorpio, ruling the reproductive system, and retrograde. With Venus ruling the 10th, it indicates that treatment has been of little help.

There was no doubt that this was a case of infertility, and I could give the client little hope for conception, which sadly was the case.

Decumbiture: Aromatherapy
2 February 2011 18:00 51N58 0E35

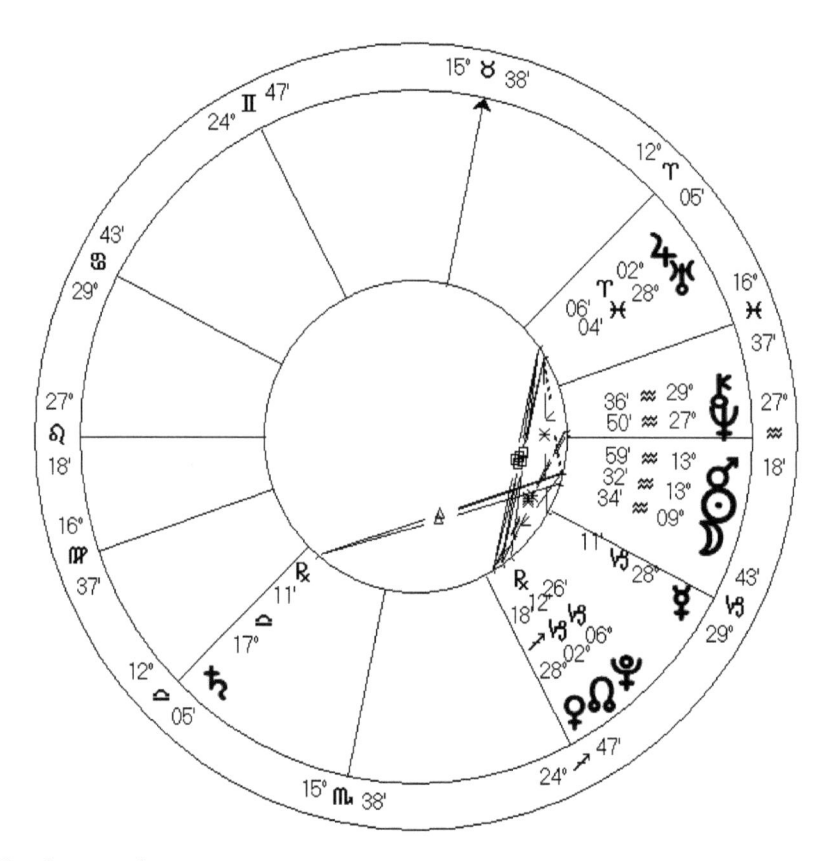

Background
Cora's presenting symptoms included painful shoulders, trapezius and deltoid muscles which she put down to her work as a hairdresser. She also suffered with high blood pressure, for which she took medication, as well as painful knees, possibly arthritis, as well as oesophagus hernia, for which she was taking medication. She was past menopausal age and suffered hot flushes at night and had difficulty sleeping. She was primarily seeking help for her aching shoulders and aching body.

Client
Leo rises so the Sun represents the client and it is in Aquarius in detriment in the 6th house which suggests the client is in a weakened position. Aquarius also refers to the circulation of the blood, it is hot and moist, and with a conjunction to Mars, describes hot flushes.

The Moon in this triple conjunction separates from Jupiter by sextile, not suggesting anything serious, a benefic aspect and benefic planet. But Jupiter is in the difficult 8th house which it rules, as well as the 5th house, so it is possible that the client has had some sort of parting, or bereavement, and a connection with children. The client was a widow and the anniversary of her husband's death was coming up soon, which is always a stressful time, and she was very concerned for her daughter's welfare at the time.

A New Moon approaches, followed by the conjunction of the Moon with Mars, the seat of the choleric humour, together with the Sun, which has its seat in the gall, linked to the digestive system. Cora is taking medication for her digestive problems.

Condition

Capricorn on the cusp of the 6th is cold and dry, with Saturn retrograde, the ruler in Libra in the 3rd house, descriptive of congestion in the shoulders.

Saturn is strong in exaltation and in its own face, stronger than the Sun, the client. The Sun however applies by trine to Saturn, which indicates a slow return to health, especially since Saturn also rules the 7th house, the physician. The brief was to help with the hot flushes, insomnia and painful shoulders and knees.

Medication: essential oils

With Taurus on the 10th house cusp, with Venus the ruler unafflicted and trine the Ascendant, I chose Geranium, thought to be a hormone balancer and helpful for menopausal problems. Since the Sun is in detriment, the heart needs a boost, so I chose Chamomile, also known as a relaxant and tonic both to heart and digestion. Neroli, a Sun oil, also helps to calm and is a tonic, as well as being helpful with insomnia.

Further treatment saw a gradual improvement in sleep patterns, hot flushes, digestion and pain in shoulders.

References
1. AA, p.17, 44th consideration.

20

Pets' Corner

Decumbiture: Visit to the Vet
31 January 2011, 9:20 am, GMT, 52N01 0E56

Background

Smokey, a grey-haired female cat, was taken to the vet to have plaque removed from her teeth. The vet's pronouncement was alarming: not all cats react well to the anaesthetic, and teeth might be lost! The chart is set for the moment Smokey entered the surgery.

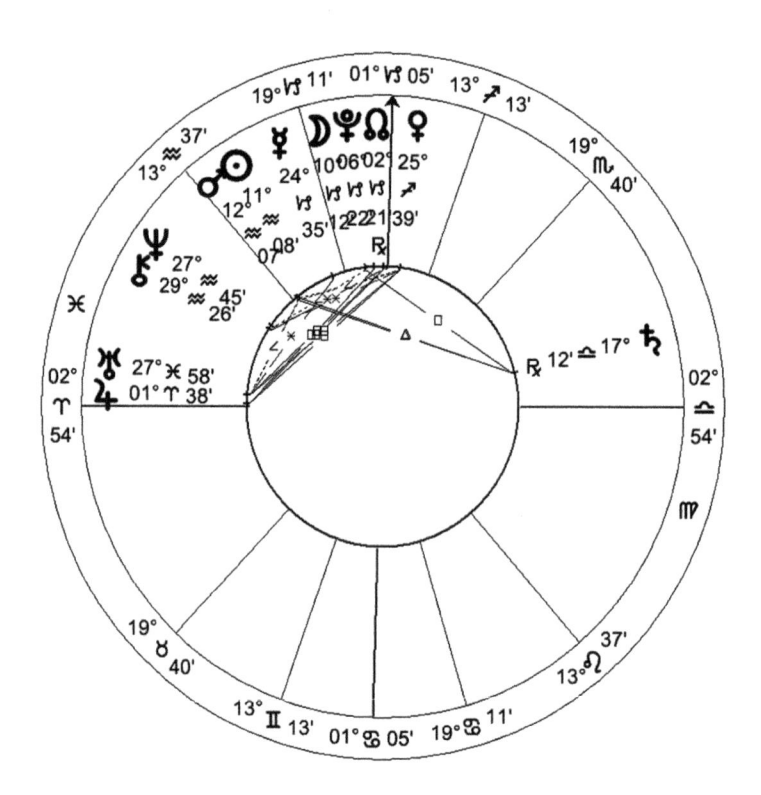

Constitution and Illness

The ruler of the hour is Jupiter, a Fortune on the Ascendant, and in its own term: a strong protective influence. Jupiter rules a benefic house, the 9th, as well as intercepted Pisces in 12th linked to hospitals - Smokey's temporary abode.

Small animals are ruled by the 6th house – this becomes Smokey's Ascendant with Leo on the cusp, appropriate for a small lion! The ruler, the Sun, is in Aquarius, its detriment, on the cusp of the 12th house; again showing a hospital environment. The Sun is strengthened slightly by exchanging face with Mercury.

Yet Smokey hadn't seemed weak at all, in fact, she seemed purrfectly well. Perhaps in this case it indicated that she had no power to affect the situation. The Sun conjunct Mars is an inflammatory combination, exacerbated by its placement in a hot and moist sign. It also opposes the 6th house cusp, Smokey's Ascendant.

Crisis

Mars is worryingly on the Part of Death, and rules the 8th house of death, as well as toxins. Yet could the combustion of Mars actually be beneficial in so much as the Sun is the cat's significator? Smokey overcomes death?

Both the Sun and Mars trine Saturn in the 7th, strong in its exaltation in Libra, though retrograde. A malefic in 7th doesn't bode well for the efficacy of the physician, especially when it rules the 10th house of medicine, but a dignified Infortune can sometimes act beneficently. Teeth, and Smokey, might be saved (Saturn ruler of Smokey's 6th house, radix 11th). This is upheld by Venus who plays the role of physician, ruling the 7th, sextile to Saturn. Edging towards the 10th house cusp, indicates that the medicine, or the operation, was appropriate.

Worrying nevertheless is the Moon, weak by detriment in Capricorn, applying with a square to Saturn.

Result

Smokey survived the small operation intact, and kept all her teeth, despite a bad case of gingivitis, an inflammatory condition of the gums caused by sticky deposit of bacteria, mucus, and food particles around the base of the teeth. (Mars conjunct Sun, inflammation, Mars ruling 8th, toxins).

As Lilly and Culpeper often say, a good aspect from the Fortunes ameliorates many a difficult situation. In this case, Jupiter, ruler of the hour is on the Ascendant and Venus is sextile Saturn, in orb traditionally. All's well that ends well.

Decumbiture: The Cat Looks Pregnant
18 February 2011, 16:53 GMT, 51N58 0E25

Background

When a two-year-old black and white cat named Lily joined the menagerie, the owner was quite unaware that she might be pregnant. Her bulging stomach and pronounced teats were at variance to her small black and white frame. She had recently suckled kittens belonging to a more neglectful cat, so the situation was uncertain. Cats are only pregnant for nine weeks.

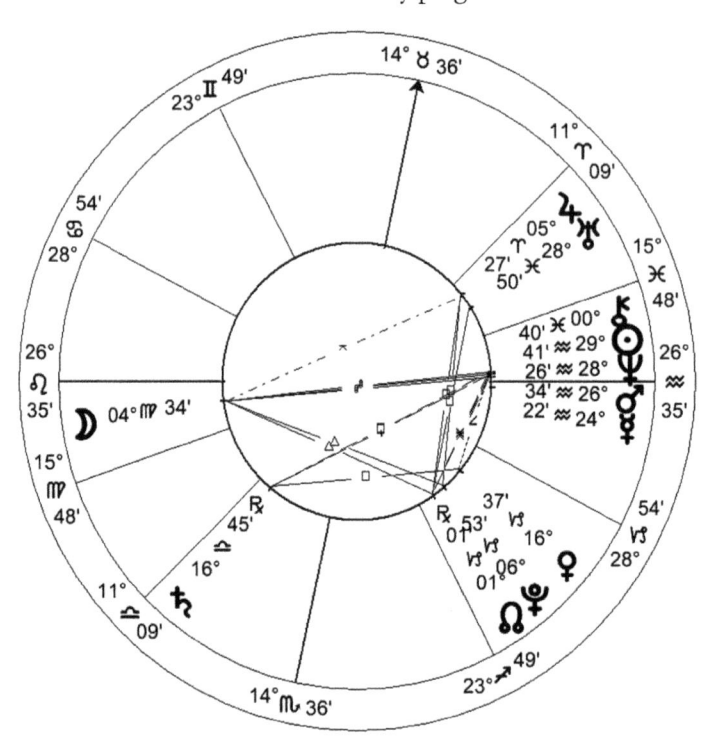

Constitution

Leo rises, relevant for an enquiry about a cat, but a malefic fixed star Adhefera conjoins the Ascendant. This is worrying, especially since the Ascendant is on the Mars/Neptune midpoint signifying weakness. Nevertheless, Jupiter ruler of the hour, fortunately rules the 5th house of progeny, except that Jupiter resides in the 8th house of death. Indeed this is descriptive of subsequent events.

The 6th house describes the cat. Capricorn on the cusp with its ruler Saturn exalted in Libra, and in its own triplicity and term, shows she is healthy. However, Saturn is retrograde suggesting problems. Saturn square Venus in the 5th is one confirmation of pregnancy since Venus rules the cat's turned 5th house (radix 10th). The planetary combination and square aspect is not conductive to an easy birth. The second indication of pregnancy is the reception between Venus and Saturn. The third, perhaps, is because Venus has joy in the 5th house.

The radix 10th house also rules medicines: would the cat need any since it is ruled by Venus? Saturn also rules the 7th house of physician: would she need one? Yes to both questions, as it turned out.

Lilly's first born, a black kitten, went walkabout because the subsequent two kittens took their time coming into the world, with much howling and wailing. He disappeared and was found much later, stone cold, limbs stiffening, almost dead. He could not suck, necessitating a trip to the vet (the physician) to bring back specially prepared milk (the medicine). Fed by syringe, he came alive, and has become an adorable easy-going cat, with no psychological hang-ups, named predictably, Blackie.

Postcript
Venus, signifying the offspring, is in the turned 12th house (radix 5th) signifying the bedroom, where they were born.

Decumbiture: Dog in Spirit
6 September 2011, 12:31 BST, 51N58 0E25

Background
The client was distraught over the death of her dog and wanted to know if he was faring well in the spirit world. Assurance could only come from describing the dog and his ailments. Time taken from the telephone call.

Client and Pet
Scorpio Ascendant for the client describes a loss or change in circumstances. The ruler, Mars in 8th house on the cusp of the 9th, confirms loss and the seeking spiritual guidance. The fixed star Pollux, linked to violence, is conjunct Mars. The client was the dog's executioner, since she had him euthanized, albeit unwillingly. Mars also rules the 12th of hospitals, or in this case, vet's surgery.

Illness
Small animals are ruled by the 6th house. Taurus on the cusp refers to the neck. The 6th house ruler, Venus in Virgo, in fall therefore weak, points to digestion. Venus rules the phlegmatic humour, linked with the lungs. Venus T-square the Nodes, indicates a genetic condition of the digestion and

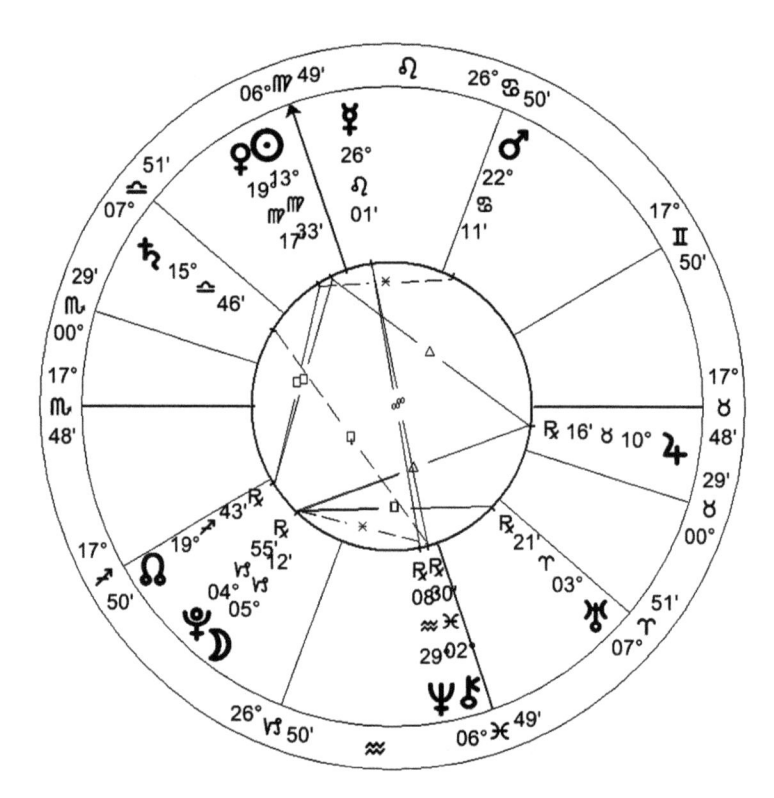

lungs. Certainly the organism is depleted since Venus is slow in motion and combust the Sun.

Also in the 6th house, Jupiter in Taurus is not releasing its benefices, since it is retrograde and on an azimene degree, as well as the Mars/Neptune midpoint, indicating a flaw in the organism and weakness. Jupiter highlights the lungs and liver. Jupiter rules the 4th house indicating the illness is with the pet until death.

The 4th house is also linked with lungs and with Chiron and Neptune on its cusp suggests dissolution of energy in the lung area, especially with Mercury in opposition. Mercury which rules the breath is on the malefic fixed star Alphard.

With the Moon trine the 6th house cusp, it was possibly a light-coloured dog. I suggested that the death was probably to do with either the lungs or the liver, and it could have been a genetic weakness.

Causes of Dog's Death
The client confirmed that the dog, a white-coloured terrier, died from faulty lungs, and that breathing problems were a weakness of the breed.

Decumbiture: Dog Bite
21 October 2011, 9:20 BST, 51N58 0E35

Background

This decumbiture illustrates how medicine may be the cause of the problem. A clash with my dog's teeth left me with punctured skin above my upper lip. By 9:20 am I was at the doctor's surgery making an appointment with the nurse for a tetanus injection.

The injection included immunization not only against tetanus but also polio and diphtheria. Close to 8 pm that evening, I began to feel feverish, very weak and unable to stand. The antibodies were in fighting form, it would seem. I went to bed and stayed there for the next two days.

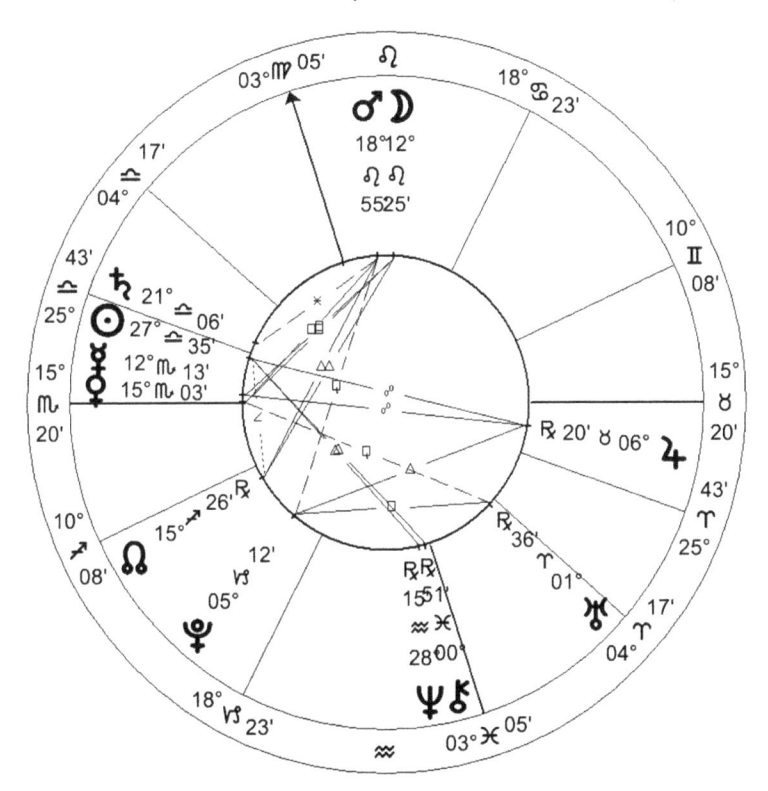

Constitution

The Moon is the ruler of the hour and is conjunct Mars, the Ascendant ruler, ruling sharp instruments (injection) and bites. Both the Moon and Mars are in Leo, suggesting heat. Scorpio rises, indicating possible toxicity, with Mars square the Ascendant, affecting the body. Mars on an azimene degree, cadent and peregrine, refers to low immunity.

Illness
Mars also rules the 6th house of illness, therefore neither patient nor illness have supremacy in strength. Small animals, i.e. the dog, are linked to this house. Aries rules the face, the site of the injury. With a late degree on the 6th cusp, the condition won't last long. Jupiter is in the 6th, a benefic supposedly helpful, but since it is retrograde and on an azimene degree, it can be problematical. Jupiter rules arterial circulation carrying the antibodies. Its opposition to Mercury, ruler of the 8th house of toxins, suggests an over-reaction to perceived bacteria. Nevertheless a trine to the MC is helpful for recovery.

Physician
Fortunately, Venus, a benefic, is conjunct the Ascendant though it's a mixed blessing since it is in detriment, but it has some strength through its own triplicity, term and angularity and it is fast in motion. Venus rules the physician (the nurse) whose intention to help inadvertently created a toxic situation. Mercury, ruler of the 10th house of medicine and also that of the 8th house of toxicity, is conjunct Venus. Mercury and Venus, reflecting toxins and physician, are square to Mars, the patient: obviously ill-suited.

Sequence of Events
The Moon separates from a square to Mercury, ruler of the 10th house of medicines as well as the 8th house of toxicity, and next applies by square to Venus, the nurse. Thereafter the Moon completes the conjunction with Mars producing an inflammatory condition: perfection of aspect came about 8pm that evening, exactly when I began to feel feverish. Next the Moon came to the sextile of an exalted Saturn, when the fever began to abate.

Decumbiture: Rabbit in Spirit
10th April 2013, 11:20 BST 51N58 00E35

Background
The client, distraught at the death of her 8-year-old pet rabbit, wondered how it fared in heaven. Only pet lovers can truly understand how deep the bond between animal and owner can be. Once again, the client's assurance of a pet heaven could only come about with description and ailment.

Pet and Owner
The Cancer Ascendant for the client, with the Part of Fortune at 23°11' Cancer conjunct the Ascendant, is quite paradoxical since the client feels

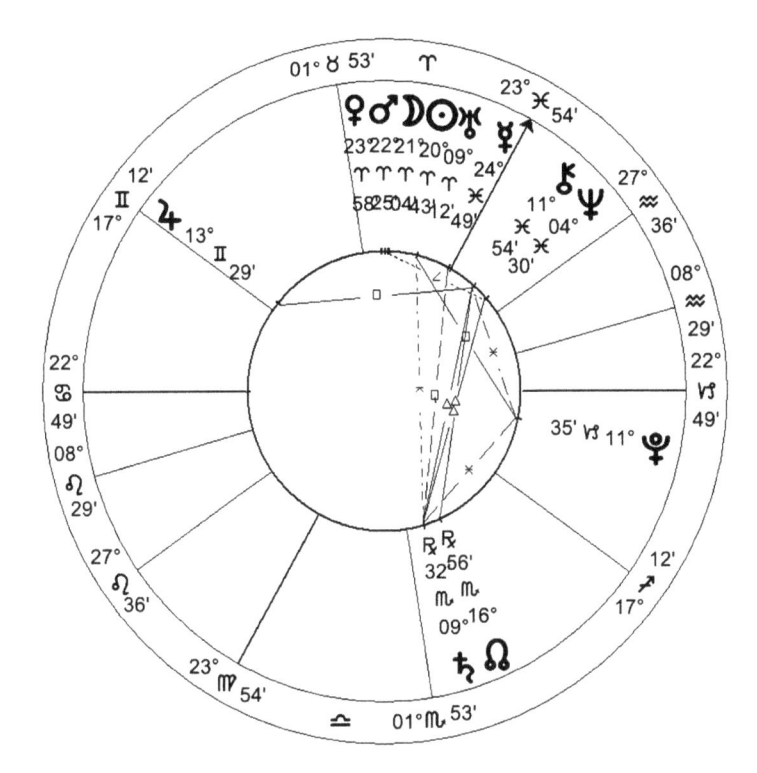

anything but fortunate. However, the ruler the Moon, as well as Mars and the Sun, are in square to the Ascendant and Part of Fortune, describing an unhappy situation. The Moon in Aries, peregrine, applying to Mars, a malefic, and ruler of the hour, describes the client's misery. A loaded 10th house is indicative of the many medicines tried and failed.

The rabbit belongs to the 6th house of small animals. With Sagittarius on cusp it well describes a four-footed beast! The ruler, Jupiter, in Gemini, in detriment and in the 12th house, shows overall weakness. Both Jupiter and Gemini are linked to the lungs and Jupiter's only aspect is a square to Chiron in Pisces, which in itself is conjunct Neptune. The Rabbit is weak, its breathing suspect.

Note that Mercury which rules the breath is in reception with Jupiter, but in detriment and fall so any help this gives is flawed.

Jupiter, opposing the 6th house cusp (the rabbit's Ascendant), shows the rabbit to have been quite large. In Gemini it could almost 'communicate' with owner. Its colour seemed like a reddish-brown, due to a mixture of planets from Aries in trine to the 6th house cusp.

Doctor and Medicine
Saturn rules the 7th house of the physician as well as the 8th house of death, and since Saturn is retrograde it doesn't look as if there was really anything he could do to save the rabbit.

Cause of Death
Assurances were gladly received since the client confirmed that the rabbit had been ailing and on the last day hardly breathing. It was a very large rabbit, light brown in colour and its eyes always followed the client, as if 'communicating' with her. The client felt somewhat reassured that the pet was somewhere hopping about in rabbit heaven.

21

Terminal Cases

Decumbiture: Friend's Illness
23 October 2011 22:15 BST 51N58 000E35

Background

News came by telephone that a friend had but a short time to live. She had incurable cancer, affecting her lungs, liver and back. She had declined further treatment which would have only prolonged her life by a few months.

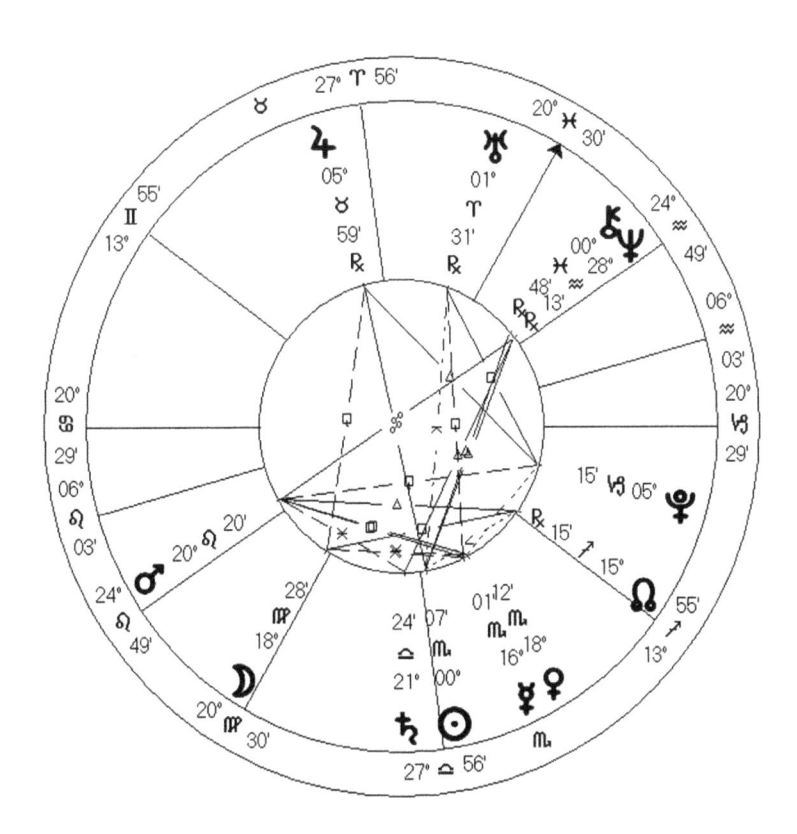

Constitution
The malefic fixed star Wasat sits on the Cancer Ascendant. Cancer relates to the digestive system, as does its ruler the Moon in Virgo. Cusping the 4th house it indicates an end to the matter, especially since it is subject to besiegement. The situation appears fated due to the T-square with the Nodes across the 6th/12th houses relating to illness and hospitalisation.

The ruler of the hour, Venus, whilst in beneficent trine to the Ascendant from the 5th house, the area of liver, back and heart, is in detriment and opposing the Part of Sickness, 10°24' Taurus. Venus conjunct Mercury - the breath - ruling the 4th house of the grave and the 12th house of hospitals. Both Mercury and Venus square Mars, a strong malefic by virtue of reception with the Sun. Venus and Mars in difficult aspect are enemies.

A strong Saturn in exaltation rules the 7th house of physicians, which might have been helpful were it not for the fact that it also rules the 8th of death. If the 8th house ruler is stronger than the Ascendant ruler, this may indicate a hard battle to regain health.[1]

Illness
Sagittarius is on the 6th house cusp, with ruler Jupiter indicative of the liver and lungs. In Taurus, Jupiter is peregrine and on an azimene degree as well as being retrograde, and clearly shows affliction. Jupiter with its sesquiquadrate aspect to the Moon puts both planets on the Mars/Saturn midpoint relating to death. The 6th house ruler is not stronger than the 1st house ruler, indicating some struggle against the illness. All planets are slow in motion as if stagnating.

Transit of Moon
The Moon entered the radix 4th house at 1.00 am the next morning. The patient went into a coma around 2.00 am and died at 11:25 am the following morning, 24th October.

Decumbiture: Taken Ill
3 November 2011, 3:00 am, 52N02 0E44

Background
A teenage girl was suddenly taken ill with acute renal failure and rushed unconscious to hospital. She was put on dialysis and initially looked as if she might pull through. She had been suffering with hypertension (high blood pressure) and kidney problems – one can often lead to the other. She was also suffering from intestinal hyperpermeability (leaky gut syndrome),

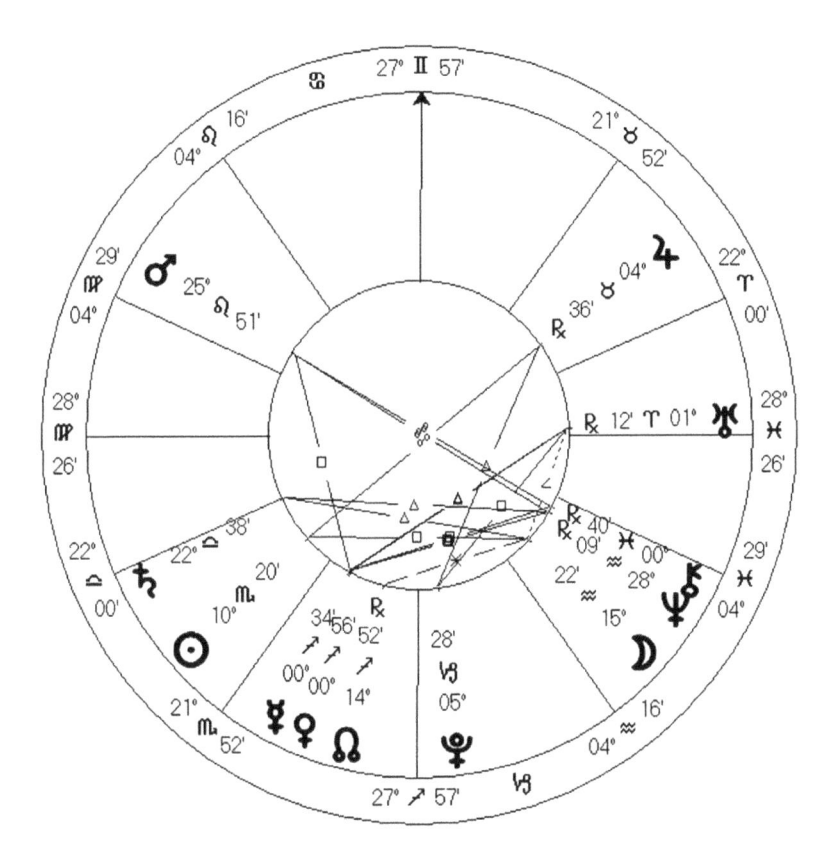

which allows toxins to permeate the gut wall, often causing an immune reaction. She drank copious amounts of water with frequent vomiting.

Constitution
A late degree of Virgo rises, often indicative of a condition nearing its end, for better or for worse. A malefic fixed star, Markab, is on the Ascendant which is also besieged by the malefics, not a good start.

Virgo is linked to the intestines and has its ruler Mercury in Sagittarius, its detriment, and in a cadent house. It also rules the 12th house of hospitals, where the patient was confined. Its conjunction to Venus, a Fortune, which is also ruler of the hour, looks positive. Venus rules the kidneys, which had been failing, but Venus shows strength by being in its own term and in reception with Jupiter, also a Fortune. Both Mercury and Venus are sextile the Ascendant. The patient is endeavouring to put up a fight for survival but it is the square from Mars to both Mercury and Venus which is damaging, as it rules the 8th house. Its degree in Leo is close to Alphard, a fixed star indicated in drowning and poisoning. This somewhat describes the lungs and gut in this case.

Illness
Sagittarius is on 6th house cusp, and its ruler Jupiter is not in the best position since it is retrograde and in the 8th house. It also rules the 7th house of physicians, and 4th house, the end of the matter The illness will be with the patient until death. It looks as if Jupiter, ruling the illness is stronger than the patient, ruled by Mercury, at least by essential dignity. Jupiter is on malefic fixed star, Sharatan, and on the antiscia of Mars, the 8th house ruler.

Jupiter opposes the Sun, whose reception with Mars is not fortunate since Mars rules the 8th house. This puts the heart, ruled by the Sun, under strain, not helped by its placement on the Mars/Saturn and Saturn/Neptune midpoint.

Passage of the Moon
The Moon is peregrine, therefore weak, but her trine to an exalted Saturn at 4:00 pm on the following afternoon gives some hope of recovery since this aspect coincided with the patient being put on a life-support machine. Unfortunately, the Moon's next contact is an opposition to Mars at 2:10 am on 4th November. Mars rules the 8th house of death. This coincided with a decision to switch off the life-support machine, due to renal failure and fluid on the lungs. The patient died a little later at 2:30 am.

Outer Planet
It is difficult to ignore Neptune as it is part of a T-square with Mercury and Venus, and Mars. The god of the waters together with Chiron describe the patient's lungs suffused with water.

Decumbiturer: Relative Dying
14 March 2013 13:45 51N58 000E35

Background
News reached me by telephone that a relative was close to death. She was 92 years old and her physical faculties were failing, although her mind was still lucid, with no sign of dementia. Ultimately, it was her lungs that were unable to function.

Constitution
Leo rises, highlighting the heart, with the Sun its ruler in Pisces, cadent in the 9th house. It is peregrine but in its joy, the patient is weak but at

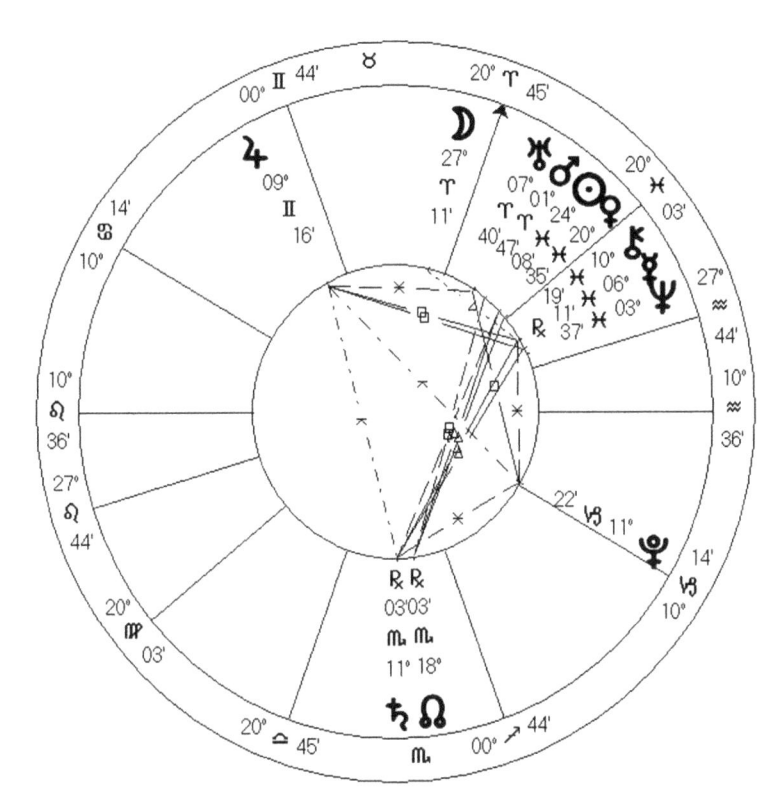

ease. The Sun puts Mars and Venus into combustion, thus weakening their intrinsic strength. Mars rules the 10th house of medicine, as does Venus (Taurus is intercepted in the 10th house). However, Venus also rules the 4th house of the grave, and perfected combustion on 17th March, the day the patient fell into a coma.

The Ascendant, representing the patient, is weakened by a square from Saturn, peregrine and retrograde. A retrograde planet from the 4th suggests congestion of the lungs. Indeed, the patient did not have the strength to cough and release phlegm. Saturn linked to the Nodes suggests a fateful situation particularly since it rules 6th, 7th and 8th, illness, physician and death.[2]

Moreover, the square between Saturn (death) and the Ascendant (life), is imminent of perfection, whereas the sextile between the Ascendant and Jupiter, which might have thrown a protective influence over the situation, is unfortunately a separating one. Benefits are unravelling it would seem, and deficits are accruing.

Jupiter is ruler of the hour and the manner of death was peaceful, surrounded by her family.

Transit of the Moon

The Moon, void of course at decumbiture, moves out of Aries (on the same day) where it has no dignity into Taurus where it is exalted and therefore strong. Its first aspect, a sextile to Mercury, which cannot help however, since the planet is in detriment, fall and retrograde. It is also in the 8th house and on the Mars/Saturn midpoint. The Moon reaches the opposition of Saturn on 15th, a danger of death, but the strength of the Moon bypasses the threat.

It then makes a sextile to Venus, the Sun and Mars, which began to look promising. The patient was reported to be smiling and happy, but passed away quite peacefully when the Moon reached the square to the natal Sun on 19th March, two days short of the first crisis day. Note that the Sun is sesquiquadrate Saturn and Ascendant: all three points triggered by the transit of the Moon.

Decumbiture: Collapse
23 May 2013 21:43 51N58 0E35

Background

News came that an acquaintance had collapsed, but not having the appropriate time of the incident, this chart was set up upon hearing that her organs had begun to fail. There was still hope, it was thought, of recovery. A heart condition was suspected.

Condition of patient

Ostensibly the chart looks hopeful for survival, but ultimately it is the lack of planetary movement that creates a static situation.

The ruler of the hour, Saturn, is not the most hopeful of planets unless dignified, which sadly is not the case. It is retrograde, halting the life force.

The Sagittarius Ascendant links to the liver and with the ruler Jupiter in detriment in Gemini, does not bode well for the organ's strength. Since Jupiter rules the lungs and arterial blood circulation, these may be suspect too. The ruler of the Ascendant in the 7th is not a good position, as it opposes the 1st house, life.

Yet the applying conjunction of Venus, a Fortune, to Jupiter, could be hopeful if it were not ruling the 6th house of illness, and 5th signifying the heart. Venus in its own term is marginally stronger than Jupiter. This suggests that the illness is stronger than the patient. Mercury, conveyor of life force, in its own sign and ruling 7th house, suggests the physicians might yet be effective. The fact that a benefic fixed star, Rigel, is conjunct both Mercury and Venus, would add weight to recovery.

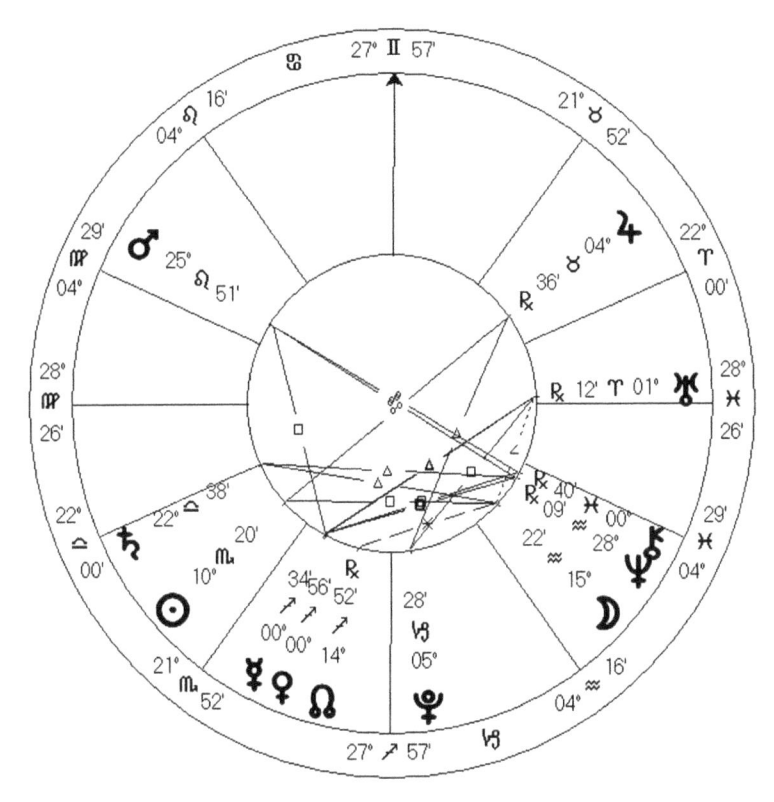

Mercury and Venus on the Mars/Uranus midpoint show the suddenness of the situation. Both planets are square Chiron in the 4th house of the grave, making a T- square with the horizon and the planets in the 7th house. Neither does Mars, ruling the 4th house, help the situation, since it is on the cusp of the 6th house. In Taurus, its detriment, it may signify a struggle with the Life Force, and is not helped by being conjunct the malefic fixed star Algol.

The Lights
It is the condition of the Lights that seal the situation. The Sun, whilst not altogether weak as it exchanges term with Jupiter, has no helpful aspects. Positioned in the 6th house, this is not a good omen for the heart.

The Moon is unfortunately very weak in this chart. It is in Scorpio, its detriment, ruling the 8th house, void of course, as well as on the Mars/Saturn midpoint. The Moon conjunct the North Node is beneficent, but unfortunately the South Node in the 5th house relating to the heart conjoins the Part of Fatality.

There is a decided lack of movement involving all planets except those in the 7th house which become isolated from the rest of the chart. Unfortunately she died on 6 June 2013 when the transit Moon passed over natal Mars, the ruler of the 4th house, the grave.

References
1. CA, p.283.
2. AJD, p.98.

22

Famous Decumbitures

Decumbiture: Nelson Mandela, Hospitalisation
25 February 2012, 9:00 am, Johannesburg 26S15 28E00

Background
News breaking on Nelson Mandela's hospitalisation was around 9:00 am, maybe a little earlier. The condition was described as a long-standing abdominal complaint, possibly a hernia, but this was not confirmed. Assurances were given by the family that the hospital visit was routine. Indeed, Nelson Mandela left the hospital within two days. How does the chart indicate a positive outcome? (Written before Nelson Mandela's death in 2013.)

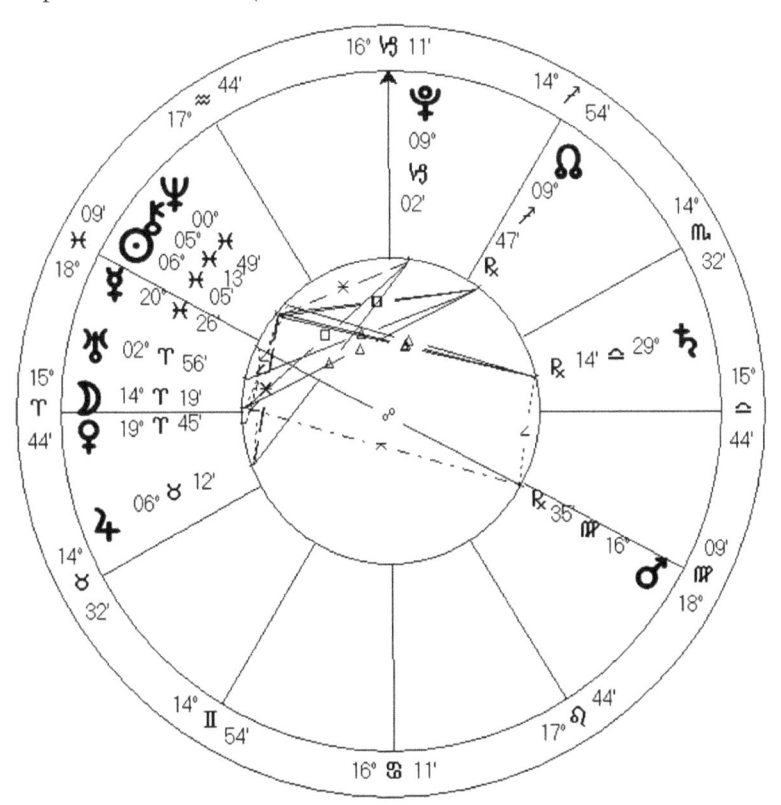

Constitution and Condition

Aries rises with the Moon placed therein and conjunct the Ascendant, ruling the 4th house of the grave, which does not look promising. The Moon does give confirmation of the 'abdominal condition' by its inconjunction to Mars, ruler of the Ascendant, and of the hour, placed in Virgo on the cusp of the 6th house. Virgo rules the abdomen, the small intestines in particular. Mars rules muscles.

A further connection exists between the Moon and Mars through antiscia, which suggests inflammation and irritation, often the result of a hernia which is a protrusion of an organ or tissue through a muscle in the abdominal wall.

Mars is peregrine and retrograde, therefore weak, and also rules the 8th house. This condition is likely to be long-standing confirmed by the opposition of Mars to Mercury, ruler of the 6th house. Since Mercury is both in detriment and fall, it appears as if the illness as well as the patient are as weak as each other. The situation, at this stage, looks problematical.

In the 1st house, we also have Jupiter influencing the constitution, which as a Fortune should be helpful, but it is peregrine and on an azimene degree. Jupiter in Taurus may point to the oesophagus by which food is carried to the stomach, indicating perhaps that it is indeed the digestive system which is in focus here.

Nevertheless, Jupiter does bring blessings and casts a sextile to the Sun, which rules the heart. It also rules 5th house linked to the heart and the Sun is strong through reception and triplicity with Venus. Overall, two Fortunes in the 1st house, no matter their actual condition, seem to favour recovery.

Time Marker

The Moon's applying conjunction to Venus, a Fortune, is a good sign of recovery, despite the latter being in detriment, but Venus is strengthened by reception with Sun as noted. Since Venus also rules the 7th house of physicians, it might be assumed that Nelson Mandela was in excellent hands.

The 10th house ruler Saturn in the 7th weakening the efficacy of physicians seems to be offset by Venus in its protective influence on the Ascendant. Saturn is strong by exaltation, but retrograde, which might suggest there is no cure, but good maintenance should extend his life as was in fact the case. Mandela lived for a further year after this illness.

Decumbiture:: Natasha Richardson, Fall
16 March 2009, 12:43 pm, Quebec, Canada. 46N49 071W14

Background
Actress Natasha Richardson suffered a fall and injured her head whilst taking a ski lesson at the Mont Tremblant Resort, Quebec, Canada. The chart is erected for the time the ski patrol put out a call to paramedics; the fall occurred moments earlier. When the paramedics arrived, Natasha Richardson said she felt fine and did not need help.

However, by mid-afternoon she began to experience severe headaches and was rushed to hospital, but two days later on 18th March she sadly died. An epidural haematoma was diagnosed due to a blunt impact to the head. She was only 45 years of age. Epidural haematoma describes a build up of blood between the dura matter, a tough outer membrane and the skull.

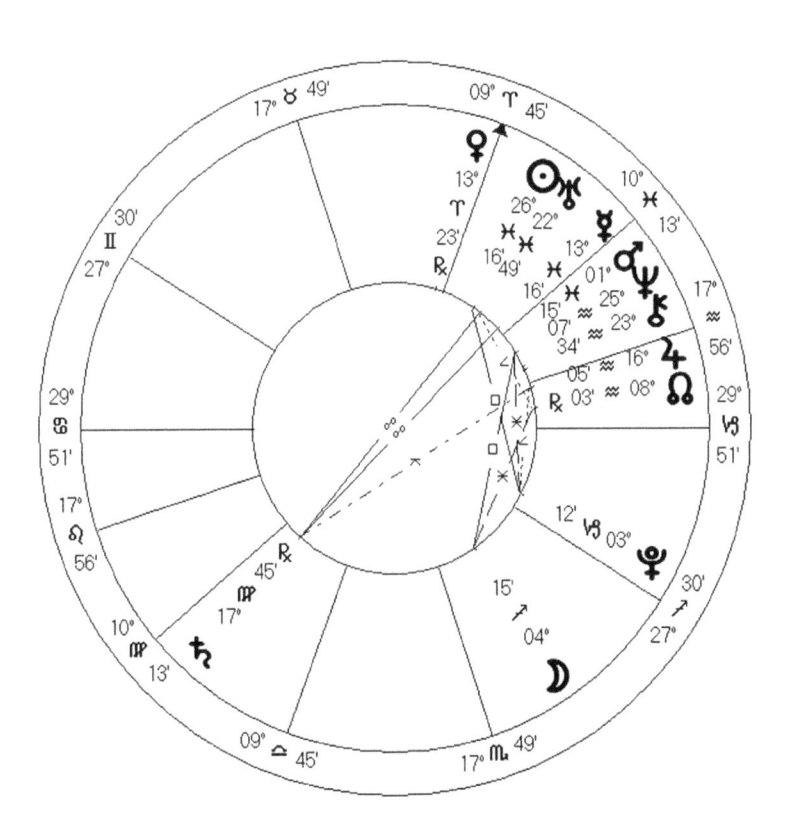

Constitution

The Cancer Ascendant represents the patient, the last degree suggesting an end to the situation for good or ill. Cancer refers to the fluids of the body, blood for instance. This sign has a link with the meninges,[1] the membranes covering the brain.

Since Leo takes up most of the 1st house, both the Sun and the Moon will represent the patient.[2] They are trine the Ascendant, and ostensibly auger well for health, but the Lights are weak. The Moon in Sagittarius in the 5th house certainly describes the activity at the time of the fall: a recreational sport. Sagittarius rules the legs and falls. The cold and moist Moon is uncomfortable in a hot and dry sign, and is peregrine, therefore has little strength. It is square Mars in the 8th house of death, and besieged by Saturn and Pluto.

The Sun's square to the 6th house cusp is not helpful. The hot and dry Sun is uncomfortable in Pisces, a cold and moist sign. Ostensibly it appears strong since it is in reception with fortunate Venus, by exaltation and triplicity.

It will be seen that Venus is powerless to help. Ruling the 4th house of the grave, she brings the spectre of death into prominence in the 10th house of medicine. That the threat may well become a reality can be seen from her debilitated condition.

Not only is she in detriment and retrograde, she is on the Mars/Neptune midpoint which relates to infection and paralysed activity. A conjunction to the Part of Fortune, had it been closer, might have helped. Instead the Part of Death at 13°31' Libra opposing her, and the Part of Sickness at 13°20' Capricorn, in square, take their toll. (Square aspects from the Arabic Parts may not be usual practice, but sometimes they cannot be ignored.)

To add insult to injury, Venus falls on the antiscium of Saturn. A meeting between the ruler of the 4th (Venus) and 8th (Saturn) creates a dire situation.[3] Venus in Aries does not auger well for this part of the body, the head, the point of impact.

The Condition

Late degree Sagittarius on the cusp of the 6th, with late degrees on the Ascendant, indicates an imminent resolution. Jupiter, the 6th house ruler, knocks on the 8th house of death, and in Aquarius refers to the blood circulation. It has no helpful traditional aspects. Pluto cannot be ignored in the 6th house especially since it squares the Sun, indicating a grievous situation and possibly irrevocable change.

The Physician
The late degree on the 7th house signals that the patient is beyond the help of physicians, something confirmed by Saturn, which rules the 7th and is peregrine and retrograde. Saturn's rulership of the 8th house creates an ominous opposition to Mercury, ruler of the hour, weak in its detriment and fall, boding ill for the nervous system. Saturn opposes the Sun, effectively weakening the vital spirits and threatening death,[4] especially since the Sun is linked to the 1st house, the constitution.

Timing of Events
The Moon in this chart is both the Ascendant ruler and describes forthcoming events as it transits the decumbiture chart.

The Moon's last aspect, a square to a peregrine Mars in Pisces in the 8th house, possibly indicates weak blood flow. Yet the Moon's next aspect, a trine to the Part of Fortune in Aries on the cusp of the 10th house, (around eight pm on same day), seems hopeful, as does its trine and sextile to the Nodes. The South Node in Leo in the 1st house however, is a detrimental position highlighting the blood circulation and the head.

The next aspect from the Moon is to the Midheaven which shows medical treatment. Natasha Richardson had been rushed to hospital and was receiving urgent medical attention.

The next aspect for the Moon is square Mercury, at around 7 am on the next day, 17 March. The weak Mercury cannot transmit the life force adequately. It gains little strength by being in its face, and is weakened by being on the Mars/Uranus midpoint which represents injury, accident and operation. Mercury as we saw earlier opposes Saturn across the 9th/3rd houses representing the nervous system. This aspect will weaken conduction of nerves. Mercury also rules the 3rd, and 12th house of self-undoing. Not everyone seeks medical treatment after receiving a bump to the head.

The transit Moon next trines Venus and sextiles Jupiter, which should have helped save the patient but as we have seen Venus has little power. Jupiter has some strength by face, but even this is not good news since Jupiter rules the 6th house of illness and is slightly stronger than the Moon, ruling the patient.

Effectively, all planets in this decumbiture chart are weak, and lack close traditional aspects. The closest aspects involve the Infortunes: Moon square Mars and Mercury opposition Saturn.

Decumbiture: Christopher Reeve, Fall
27 May 1995 15:05 Culpeper, Virginia. 38N28.23 77W59 49

Background

Christopher Reeve fell from his horse in a riding competition and severed the first and second vertebrae in his neck. He did not breathe for three minutes before paramedics arrived on the scene. His life was saved but the injury left him paralyzed from the neck down. He lived for nine more years though confined to a wheelchair, his breathing aided by oxygen apparatus.

Constitution

Libra rises, perhaps indicating life in the balance. The Ascendant degree receives a trine from the Sun, as well as Uranus, suggesting strength of constitution. This is upheld by Venus, the Ascendant ruler in domicile, as well as in its own triplicity. In Taurus, it points to the neck, and in the 8th house, a crisis or loss, or death. Since Venus makes no applying aspect to another planet, its movement is somewhat curtailed, but it does trine the

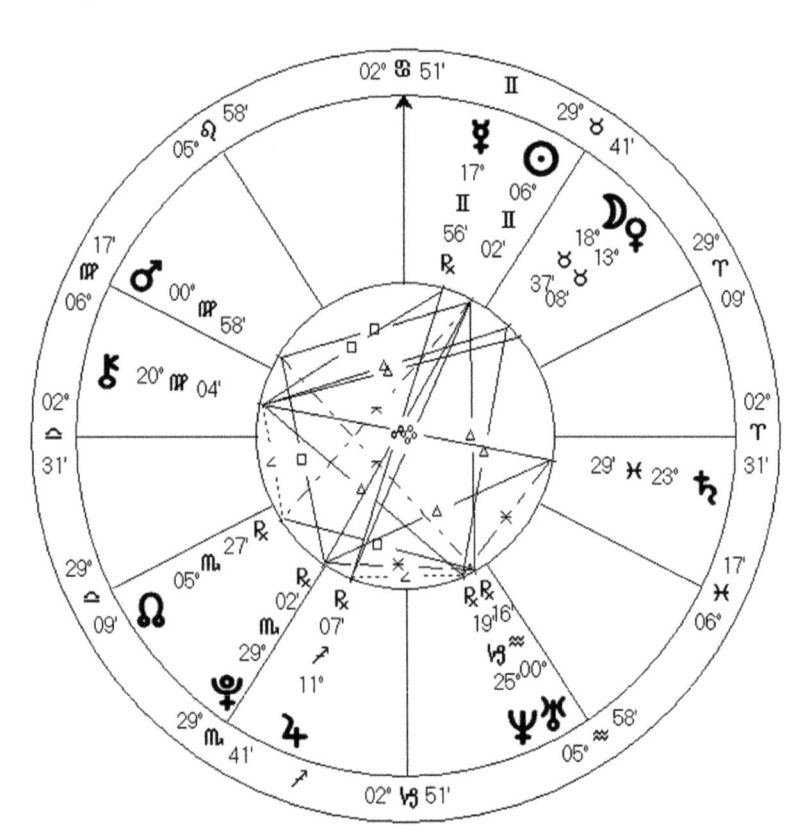

Part of Fortune in Virgo in the 12th house, pointing to beneficial treatment in hospital. Venus on the midpoint of 'accident', Mars/Uranus, is descriptive, and also indicates medical intervention.

The Moon, conjunct Venus, in Taurus is strong in exaltation and rules the 10th house of medicine. It separates from a conjunction of Venus and applies by sextile to Saturn in Pisces in the 6th house of illness. Saturn in 6th is deleterious but its position is mitigated by the sextile from a Fortune. But limitation is by Saturn's opposition to Chiron in the 12th house. Saturn, which has no dignity, is also ruler of the hour, descriptive of falls and suggesting a grievous illness.

Saturn also rules the 5th house indicating the back and the heart, so illness will affect these areas. Saturn's rulership of the 4th indicates a condition until death.

Condition

Pisces, a mutable sign on the 6th house cusp in an early degree shows the beginning of an illness, and a fluctuating condition. Over the next few years Christopher Reeve was pulled back from the brink of death several times. The 6th house ruler, Jupiter in Sagittarius in the 3rd house, is also descriptive of the event – a fall from a horse. Jupiter is retrograde, stemming the life force, and opposing the Sun in Gemini, creating difficulties with the nervous system. Mercury in Gemini, linked to the nervous system, is strong but retrograde, therefore the life force is not flowing smoothly. This is upheld by the square to Saturn. Christopher Reeve required breathing apparatus until the end of his life.

Nevertheless, the comparison of strength between Venus and Jupiter, constitution and illness respectively, comes down on the side of Venus. Christopher Reeve lived for another nine years, albeit confined to a wheelchair.

Doctors and Medicine

Mars ruling the 7th house is peregrine, indicating that physicians were unable to help, although the Moon ruling the 10th of medicine is strong by exaltation, describing excellent medication. It seems a little contradictory. Indeed, his life was saved because of surgery to reconnect the neck vertebrae which had been severed from the rest of the spine. The weak Mars relating to the physicians, may be suggesting that a full cure was not possible.

Christopher Reeve spent the rest of his life filming and lobbying on behalf of people with spinal-cord injuries and for human embryonic stem cell research, founding the Christopher and Dana Reeve Foundation.

Death

The strength of the Ascendant ruler Venus, as well as the Moon, may well have helped him to fight off the series of near-fatal infections over the years before his ultimate death. He died on 10 October 2004 of cardiac arrest, purportedly caused by adverse reaction to an antibiotic.

The planet Pluto is thought to be linked to antibiotics (action is to kill bacteria). At the time of his death transiting Pluto at 20° Sagittarius activated the T-square with Chiron, Mercury and Saturn in the decumbiture chart, which would have affected the nervous system.[5] Interestingly, Saturn (ruling the 4th house of the grave in the decumbiture chart) reached the opposition to the Ascendant and square to the Midheaven by solar arc nine years from the accident.

Decumbiture: Abraham Lincoln, Assassination
14 April 1865, 22:25, Washington, VA. 38N42.46 78W09.35

Background

If we see a decumbiture chart as representing the moment someone is no longer able to function in a healthy condition, or execute their normal activities through the lowering or absence of the life force, then it is possible an outside threat to health may also qualify for this kind of chart, and can be read by similar rules.

One example was the assassination of President Abraham Lincoln by well-known actor, and Confederate spy, John Wilkes Booth. This occurred on the 14th April 1865 at around 10:25 pm during a theatre performance in Washington DC. Slumped forward in the chair after being shot in the head near the left ear, the president was then lowered on to the floor by Dr Charles Leale, a young Army surgeon who had also been attending the play.

The president initially had no pulse but after a clot of blood was removed from the wound, his breathing improved. Another doctor in the audience, Dr Albert King, helped to carry Lincoln's body across the street to a boarding house where they laid him diagonally on the bed because he was too tall to lie straight. There were many physicians in attendance but he breathed his last just nine hours later on 15 April 1865 at 7.22 am.

Constitution

The Moon, the ruler of the hour, and of the 8th house, cusps the Ascendant, threatening death.[6] Injury is grave since the Moon is on the malefic fixed star Antares, with a dearth of aspects.

Sagittarius rises describing the exceptionally tall Lincoln, a lawyer.

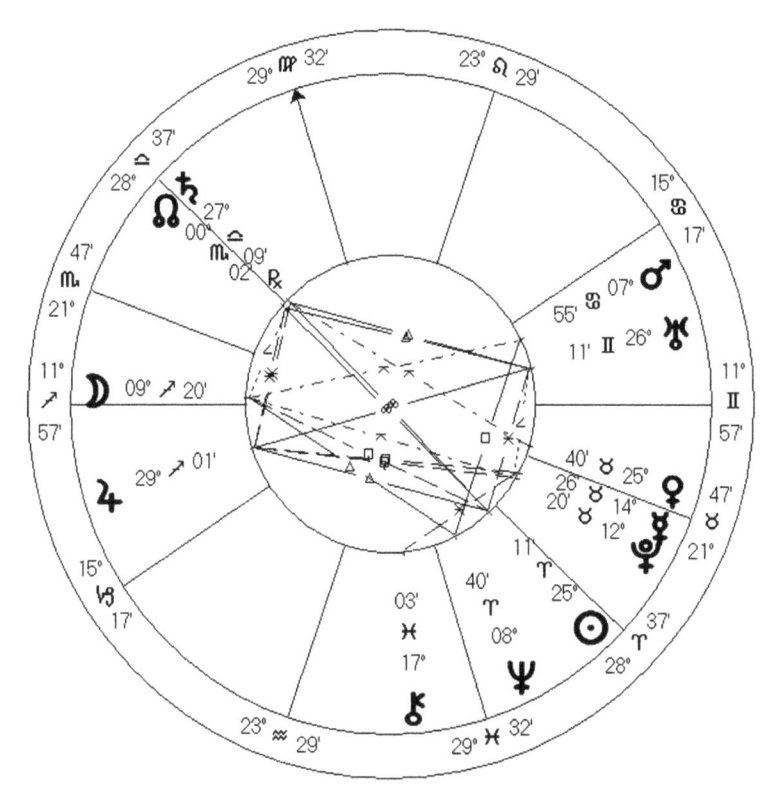

Jupiter, ruler of the Ascendant, representing the President's health and constitution, appears strong since it is in domicile. But exchanging term with Mars and face with Saturn, both malefics, is a dubious strength.

Jupiter has more glories since it receives an applying trine from a strong Sun in exaltation. This Sun is conjunct the Part of Fortune and in a congenial sign. The President was in good spirits. It was five days after the surrender of the Confederate army, and victory in the Civil War was almost assured.

But this rosy picture is spoilt by the South Node close to the Sun and opposite a strong Saturn in exaltation. Being retrograde, Saturn uncharacteristically 'hastens' to the opposition of the Sun, before the Sun can perfect the trine to Jupiter.

A malefic fixed star, Sinistra, conjoins Jupiter, and since Jupiter also rules the 4th house, the grave beckons. Further, Jupiter has stationed and will retrograde during the next few hours, halting the life force.

Breakdown in Health
The 6th house further describes disruption to the life force, with Taurus on the cusp and Venus ruler strong in domicile in the 6th. A conjunction to

the fixed star Algol however, spoils hope. Algol has links with decapitation which describes the wound to the head and symbolises the nation losing its head of state.

Physician and Medicine
The fixed star Aldebaran, a malefic, in Gemini on the 7th house cusp, with Mercury the ruler in the 5th, describes where the crime took place - a theatre - and where treatment was administered. Mercury has strength by being in its own term and exchanging face with the Moon, but there are no traditional aspects to support the actions. Despite the physicians' every effort, they were unable to help. Mercury also rules the 10th house of medicine.

Death
Description of the assailant may be represented by Mars, as Scorpio is on the cusp of the 12th house of secret enemies. Mars in detriment in Cancer in the house of open enemies, is weak but gains some strength by exchanging term with Jupiter (culprit and victim) and being fast in motion. After Booth shot the President he fled the theatre but was caught almost two weeks later and shot in the head. Mars is close to fixed star Alhena, linked to wounds. Mars also rules the 5th house, describing Booth, an actor by profession.

Timing by the Moon
The Moon makes no aspect before Jupiter turns retrograde during the early hours of the next day, 15th April. The President breathed his last at 7.22 am.

Decumbiture: Rudolph Valentino, Collapse
23 August 1926, 11:50 New York, 40N40 73W56

Background
Extraordinarily popular silent film star Rudolph Valentino collapsed in a hotel lobby in New York on 15th August 1926 at 11:50 am, and died eight days later on 23rd August 1923 at 12.10 pm. The New York Times recorded the time. The renowned American astrologer Evangeline Adams apparently predicted the demise of the famous movie star by using a decumbiture chart (Placidus house).*

---

* Joseph Silveiro de Mello includes Valentino's decumbiture chart in his book *Decumbitures and Diurnals*, AFA, 2003, and an article appeared in *The Traditional Astrologer*, Issue 14, May 1997 on decumbitures by Karen Christino.

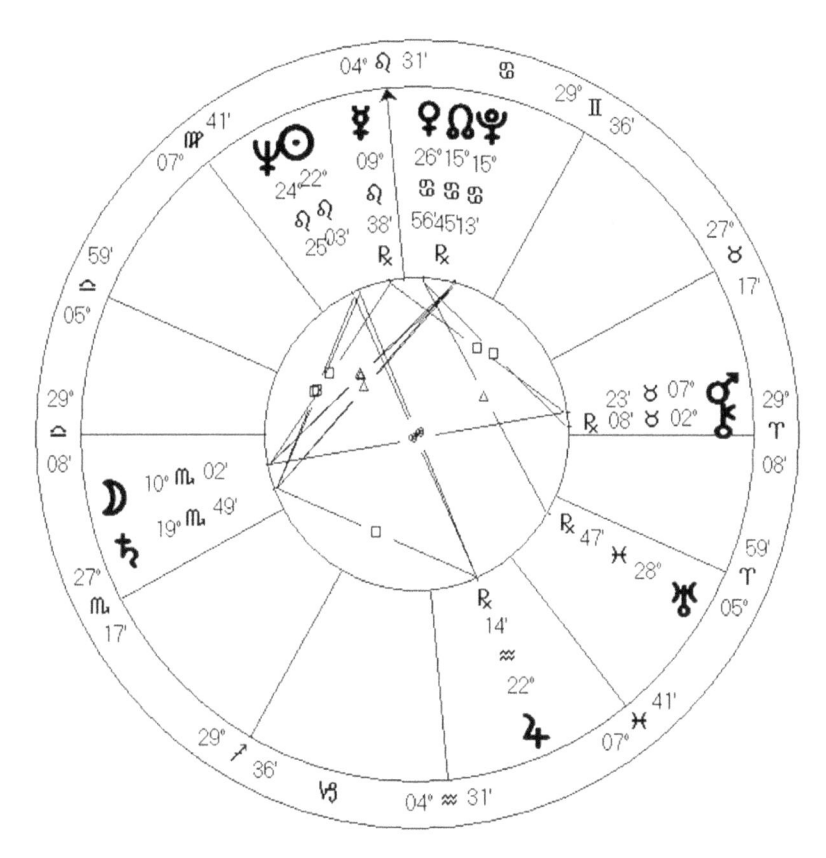

Valentino had severe abdominal pains, which under X-ray revealed a large perforated gastric ulcer as well as appendicitis (acute inflammation of the appendix, a narrow tube that branches of the intestine, containing lymphoid tissue). After an operation, Valentino showed signs of recovery, but his condition deteriorated on the sixth day and by the eighth, he was dead. He developed peritonitis, inflammation of the lining of the abdominal cavity, a toxic condition sometimes following appendicitis. In his weakened condition, pleurisy set in (inflammation of the pleura, the membrane lining the lungs), which made breathing painful.

Constitution

There is no record apparently of Ms Adams' actual analysis of the decumbiture, so it might be interesting to try to see how she arrived at the death being on the eighth day. The last degree of Libra rises indicating that the matter is nearing its end, for good or ill. Venus, the Ascendant ruler, in Cancer, is also far along in the sign, confirming matters drawing to a close. Venus is strong by essential dignity since it is in its own triplicity and term, and therefore the patient is also strong, ostensibly. However, the following weaken Venus:

> 1) She also rules the 8th and 12th houses: death and confinement (hospitalisation).
> 2) Venus is also in an intercepted sign in the 9th house, suggesting confinement again.
> 3) Further, Venus does not make helpful aspects.
> 4) Venus, cold and moist, is comfortable in Cancer, but entered Leo (a hot and dry sign) three days later on 17 August, worsening the condition.
> 5) Venus was also opposing the Part of Fatality at 26°51' Capricorn.

Mars and Saturn in the 1st house are both peregrine and therefore weak. Malefic planets in the Ascendant threaten death.[7]

The Disease and Physicians

So what of the disease? Aries on 6th house cusp suggests inflammation since it rules the choleric humour, which has its seat in Mars, and is of course the planetary ruler of Aries. The choleric humour rules gall or yellow bile, a greenish-brown fluid formed from waste products in the liver, which is ultimately discharged into the small intestine. That there is something awry with this process is suggested by the afflicted Mars in Taurus which rules the oesophagus by which food is transported through the digestive tract. Taurus is in detriment (weak), peregrine (weak) and conjunct Chiron (a wound). To compound matters Mars at 7° Taurus is on an azimene degree as well as on a violent fixed star, Hamal, at 7°40' Taurus.

Normally, if the ruler of the 6th house is weak and that of the Ascendant is strong, the patient has the strength to overcome the disease. Unhappily not in this case, because the weak Mars also rules the 7th house of physicians and is in the 7th house, so it reduces their efficacy. 'If an Infortune is in the 7th, we have paltry physicians'.[8] If that wasn't enough, the Part of Death (16°15' Taurus) is in the 7th house.

The physicians might well have done all they could within their means, but there were no life-saving antibiotics in early 20th century. Yet the Sun, which rules the 10th house of medicine, is in Leo and therefore strong in its own sign, as well as in its own triplicity. Afflicted by the square to Saturn, the opposition of Jupiter and the conjunction with Neptune, its strength was sapped.

Time Markers

The Moon is badly placed in its fall in Scorpio. Worse still, the Moon is conjunct Saturn and in aspect to the ruler of the 6th house Mars. Indeed, the Moon had separated from the Mars/Mercury square. Mercury is not without dignity, being in its own term, but its retrograde motion in the 10th house of medicine suggests stagnation. Mercury also rules the vital force, and when this is disturbed there is an imbalance in health. The engine has no power.

Within a few hours of Valentino's collapse the Moon reached a sextile to the Part of Fortune (17°04' Capricorn) and a trine to the North Node, signifying the great hopes for recovery. However, not for long: the Moon perfected the conjunction to Saturn soon after. Saturn rules membranes and it is the peritoneum membrane that became inflamed. Nevertheless Valentino did not die at this point because the Moon is also trine Venus, a Fortune, which is a mitigating factor.[9]

However, when the transiting Moon reached its first crisis day seven days later on 22nd August, in Aquarius, it set off the T-square with Jupiter, Saturn, Sun and Neptune. The Sun and Jupiter are also on the illness midpoint, Saturn/Neptune. If the Moon is in aspect to both a Fortune and Infortune, such as Jupiter and Saturn, a conflict arises. Jupiter endeavours to maintain health, whilst Saturn strives to destroy it. Usually, it is the stronger planet that overcomes the weaker.[10] Jupiter in its own term, is only marginally stronger than peregrine Saturn. Unfortunately Jupiter is retrograde and cannot utilise its strength against Saturn. Saturn, ruler of the hour, rules the 4th house, the grave, and there is possibility of death if the Moon afflicts the ruler of the grave.[11] The transiting Moon opposes the Sun - a Full Moon - bringing the situation to fruition, for good or ill.[12]

Quick Resolution

Apparently, an illness occurring in the summer is short, for good or ill. Cardinal signs, which represent days, are on the sixth house cusp and the Ascendant, and Venus the Ascendant ruler is placed in cardinal Cancer. Mars, the ruler of the sixth, is placed in fixed Taurus but in an angular house, which also represents days.

Valentino should have died on the 22nd August 1926, around midnight, when the Moon set off the above T-square, but he actually breathed his last twelve hours later. He was unconscious for most of the 23rd so we can say he was already 'dead to the world'.

It is interesting however that the decumbiture Ascendant at 29°04' Libra reached the opposition to Mars in Scorpio 7°23' in 8°19' minutes, which symbolically speaking would bring us to 23rd August 1926. These days it would be unethical to predict death, so all one could say is that the 22nd would have been a day of serious crisis.

Decumbiture: First Triple Transplant*
21 January 2012, 3:15 am, Antalya, Turkey, 36N53 30E42

Background

Atilla Kavdir aged thirty-four, made medical history by having the first triple transplant performed in Akdeniz University Hospital in Antalya, southern Turkey. He was accidentally electrocuted aged eleven and tragically lost both arms and a leg. The 25-strong team began the transplant operation at 3:15 am, after receiving the donor limbs. It is vital to keep to a minimum the time the organ is left without a normal blood supply. The operation took around eleven/twelve hours. Although the patient survived the operation and was doing well, unfortunately, due to tissue incompatibility, the leg had to be removed the next day.

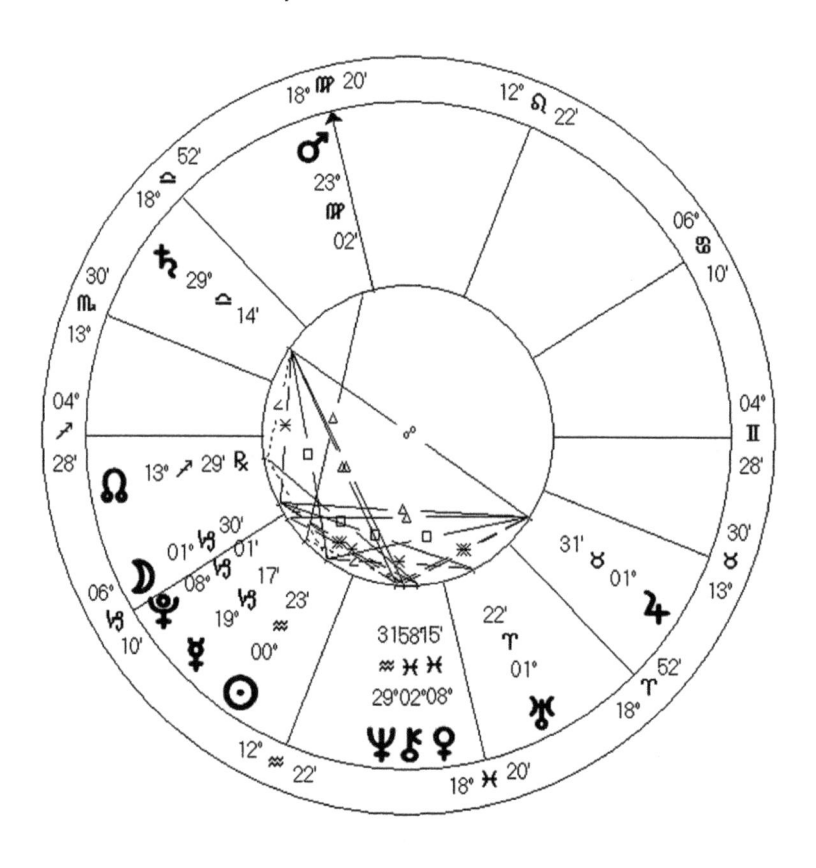

---

* Source: cbcnews.com, arab.news.com, Sunday Express 22/1/2012.

Constitution and Illness

The cosmic indications initially seem hopeful. Sagittarius, a double-bodied sign, rises; it rules the limbs, specifically the legs.

The Ascendant ruler, Jupiter in Taurus in the 5th house, points to the neck and heart, certainly the latter organ may be suspect since Jupiter is in a T-square with the Sun and Saturn. Jupiter appears strong due to reception and terms with Venus. Unfortunately Venus is the ruler of the 6th house, and strong by exaltation, slightly stronger than Jupiter. Venus in Pisces points to the immune system. Venus in triple conjunction with Chiron and Neptune is square to the Ascendant, forming a midpoint which suggests weakened glandular function.[13] This may be linked to the lymphatic system, part of the immune system, which releases white blood cells to ward off infection and reject foreign cells.

Further, Venus is square the Part of Death (9°08' Gemini) which is in the 7th house of physicians, effectively making a T-square with the Ascendant. This may not necessarily mean the death of the patient but the failure of the transplant, or part of the transplant.

Physician

Gemini is on the 7th house cusp. Mercury rules the physician and is strong by mixed reception with Mars, the latter in the 10th house of medicine.

Time Marker

The Moon marking events is not strong since it is in detriment, though it is in its own triplicity. It also rules the 8th house of death, although in this case the Moon as an indicator of developments is quite appropriate since the death of another body had to occur for the transplant to take place. The Moon is two days away from a New Moon, which is not the best time for an operation (it may cause inflammation as opposed to the Full Moon which may cause haemorrhage). Not that there is usually any choice of date in a transplant operation. Although the Moon is in the 1st house and will also represent the patient, it is within five degrees of the 2nd house cusp and will also link into the life force or energy of the patient. Strength is not on the patient's side.

Interestingly, the Moon's last aspect is a square to Uranus, describing what has gone before, and since Uranus rules electricity it is symbolic of the tragedy which occurred in the patient's youth. Uranus is also on the Saturn/Neptune midpoint, indicated in illness. The Moon's last aspect to a traditional planet was a sextile to Saturn which suggests fortitude in sickness.

Almost immediately the first applying aspect the Moon makes is a trine to Jupiter, which has a protective influence over the patient. The Moon then conjoins the Part of Fortune, which again looks beneficial, but soon enough the Moon conjoins Pluto later the same evening which signals rejection.[14] Next day the physicians had to remove the leg due to tissue incompatibility.

The patient lived until May 2012 and died of heart and kidney failure threatened by the T-square by Jupiter, Saturn and the Sun. Since the patient was still under observation within a month of the decumbiture, it is the Sun which takes over as the time marker. In May 2012 it was in the early degrees of Taurus and triggered the aforementioned T- square.

References
1. DMA, p.49.
2. BI, p.279.
3. CA, p.256.
4. CA, p. 257.
5. CSI, p.122.
6. AJD, p.105.
7. AJD, p.72.
8. AJD, p.72.
9. AJD, p.68.
10. AJD, p.106.
11. AJD, p.41.
12. EMA, p.548.
13. CSI, p144.
14. HAR, p.47.

Conclusion

A decumbiture may be compared to an event chart but differs in that it is specifically appertaining to health. It can also be likened to a horary Chart with its various rules and regulations, but some of the strictures which apply to horary, might be waived in a decumbiture, or at least woven into the fabric of delineation and judgement.

Decumbiture, like horary, has certain rules which can shed light on a perceived breakdown in health, and not necessarily when the patient has succumbed to a horizontal position. As we have seen, a decumbiture is relevant in any situation where there is an actual or even perceived disruption of the Life Force. From Culpeper's sample chart it will be quite evident that the time taken for decumbiture did not always apply to a patient taking to their bed. The young man suffering the sword wound had probably been carousing in the streets as students were, or perhaps are still wont to do.

In the 21st century we do not have the same freedom of medical diagnosis as that enjoyed by earlier astrologers. The constraints of medical ethics, since for the most part we are not physicians, halt dire pronouncements; in short, care is needed regarding the information imparted to the client, not only because we cannot be absolutely certain of the final astrological judgement, but it is imperative to leave the client/patient with hope.

Whilst conscious of the fact that a decumbiutre is not intended to take the place of orthodox medical treatment, its cosmic picture can be viewed in terms of guidance and interest. Whilst the 1st and 6th houses are familiar in terms of constitution and sickness respectively, the other houses may appear a little strange, such as the 7th house for the physician and the 10th house for the medicine. We know also, and all too well, that the 8th house has a link with death, or perhaps a toxic condition, the 4th might indeed show the grave or the end of the matter, and the 12th confinement. We must not forget that the psychological content may underlie the illness or condition. Physicians, even when medical ethics were much more lax, must have to some extent cultivated a 'bedside manner', and offered some counselling to soothe the troubled soul.

The zodiac signs in the decumbiture are linked to physiological systems and illness, as indeed are the planets. Examination of the planets may be more intricate than in natal astrology as their dignities and debilities, as well as their motion, their humoural comfort and even their planetary friendships often play a large part in judgement. The Moon particularly is important in delineation as its fast motion compared to the other planets often shows the condition altering for good or ill.

Some ideas may be turned on their head. The benefics, Venus and Jupiter, are not always fortunate, and the malefics, Mars and Saturn, are not always unfortunate. It is how the planets are configured in the signs and houses, in as much are they strong or weak therein, what aspects they make to each other that take them down a benefic or malefic path. Fixed stars, antiscia, Arabic Parts and azimene degrees may not be a crucial part of delineation, but can be an aid where judgement needs supplementary help.

As with any astrological chart – natal or horary for instance – there are always conflicting messages, and arriving at judgement is no easy matter. The patient has a fighting chance for improvement if the Sun, Moon, and Mercury are strong, the Ascendant ruler is stronger than the 6th or 8th house ruler, and the benefics are stronger than the malefics.

Planetary movement needs to be observed, aspectual perfection with another planet, perhaps turning retrograde, or moving into an uncongenial house or sign. The outer planets are not considered by many traditional astrologers, but it would be a mistake to ignore them in a health chart when prominent, as they may indeed lend valuable information.

Delineation can become quite complex especially when looking at *'What members in mans body every planet signifieth in any of the twelve signes'* according to William Lilly in Chapter 9. This can be included in judgement if there is lack of clarity in a straightforward judgement, otherwise it might create confusion.

The humours, which once constituted the backbone of medical diagnosis and treatment, are no longer held valid by the medical establishment. Who are we to argue if not medically qualified? But perhaps knowledge of the humours may serve as a possible aid in astrological judgement, and even constitute an aid to advice, or in which direction to seek advice.

Timing and length of disease can be helpful naturally, though ultimately one has to take all the various factors into consideration before there can be any judgement. Maybe the main idea to remember is that a chart influenced by the benefics may bring a shorter illness than one where the malefics have ascendancy.

The chapters on plants, aromatics and crystals are a guide to traditional rulerships which can serve as signposts to treatment, if the astrologer is in a position to do so. The smell, colour, structure as well as action upon the body of plants, and crystals likewise to some extent, were once central to planetary association. Judgement as always has to rest with the astrologer.

The chapter on Steps to Judgement is a guide and two diagrams are given to help the astrologer to keep a record of the cosmic state of the signs, planets and the movement of the Moon. The steps to judgement however are for guidance, since once the initial steps are taken the journey to delineation can take a detour into different directions. The case histories give an indication of the various circumstances under which a decumbiture may be erected. Known events which constitute a decumbiture chart are presented so that the movement of planets can be tested against the final outcome.

At the end of most chapters there are usually a set of questions posed for revision. These are also part of my course in decumbiture; please apply to the author for further details if you are interested to take things further.

Wanda Sellar
wanda.sellar@virgin.net

DISCLAIMER

The material in this book *'Introduction to Decumbiture Astrology'*, is for historical interest and study purposes only, and is not intended to take the place of orthodox medical treatment.

Titles from The Wessex Astrologer
www.wessexastrologer.com

Martin Davis	Astrolocality Astrology From Here to There	*Joseph Crane*	Astrological Roots: The Hellenistic Legacy Between Fortune and Providence
Wanda Sellar	The Consultation Chart An Introduction to Medical Astrology Decumbiture	*Komilla Sutton*	The Essentials of Vedic Astrology The Lunar Nodes Personal Panchanga The Nakshatras
Geoffrey Cornelius	The Moment of Astrology		
Darrelyn Gunzburg	Life After Grief AstroGraphology: The Hidden Link between your Horoscope and your Handwriting	*Anthony Louis*	The Art of Forecasting using Solar Returns
		Lorna Green	Your Horoscope in Your Hands
Paul F. Newman	You're not a Person - Just a Birthchart Declination: The Steps of the Sun Luna: The Book of the Moon	*Martin Gansten*	Primary Directions
		Reina James	All the Sun Goes Round
		Oscar Hofman	Classical Medical Astrology
Jamie Macphail	Astrology and the Causes of War	*Bernadette Brady*	Astrology, A Place in Chaos Star and Planet Combinations
Deborah Houlding	The Houses: Temples of the Sky		
Dorian Geiseler Greenbaum	Temperament: Astrology's Forgotten Key	*Richard Idemon*	The Magic Thread Through the Looking Glass
Howard Sasportas	The Gods of Change	*Nick Campion*	The Book of World Horoscopes
Patricia L. Walsh	Understanding Karmic Complexes		
M. Kelly Hunter	Living Lilith	*Judy Hall*	Patterns of the Past Karmic Connections Good Vibrations The Soulmate Myth The Book of Why Book of Psychic Development
Barbara Dunn	Horary Astrology Re-Examined		
Deva Green	Evolutionary Astrology		
Jeff Green	Pluto 1 Pluto 2 Essays on Evolutionary Astrology (edited by Deva Green)	*John Gadbury*	The Nativity of the Late King Charles
		Neil D. Paris	Surfing your Solar Cycles
Dolores Ashcroft-Nowicki and Stephanie V. Norris	The Door Unlocked: An Astrological Insight into Initiation	*Michele Finey*	The Sacred Dance of Venus and Mars
		David Hamblin	The Spirit of Numbers
Martha Betz	The Betz Placidus Table of Houses	*Dennis Elwell*	Cosmic Loom
		Gillian Helfgott	The Insightful Turtle
Greg Bogart	Astrology and Meditation	*Christina Rose*	The Tapestry of Planetary Phases
Kim Farnell	Flirting with the Zodiac		

Lightning Source UK Ltd.
Milton Keynes UK
UKHW02f1913231018
331051UK00003B/110/P